Nancy Chaput (802) 734-1378
purpleschoolvt@yahoo.com

Spelling for Writers

Mary Jo Fresch • Aileen Wheaton

Teacher's Edition
Grade 4

GREAT SOURCE
EDUCATION GROUP
A Division of Houghton Mifflin Company

Mary Jo Fresch previously taught third grade and Adult Literacy classes. She taught children's literature and literacy courses in teacher education programs in Ohio, Nebraska, and Melbourne, Australia. She received her Ph.D. from The Ohio State University, where she is currently an Associate Professor in the College of Education. She resides in Dublin, Ohio, with her husband, Hank. She has two children, Michael and Angela (and son-in-law Nathan Thompson).

Aileen Ford Wheaton previously was a primary and intermediate elementary classroom teacher. After years in the classroom, Aileen became a district Literacy Intervention Specialist. She also taught pre-school, adult literacy classes, G.E.D., and English as a Second Language. A native of North Dakota, Aileen currently resides in Columbus, Ohio with her husband, Jim. She has two sons, Michael and Andrew (and daughter-in-law Katie).

International Standard Book Number: 0-669-51751-8

1 2 3 4 5 6 7 8 9 10 - BA – 10 09 08 07 06 05

Contents

Lessons

Introducing

Spelling for Writers

Spelling for Writers provides a manageable way for students to explore the English language; develop numerous strategies; develop their ability to look at, listen to, and think about words; and, finally, to extend that learning into becoming fluent writers. The title of this program, *Spelling for Writers*, tells it all. We no longer assign spelling, we teach children how to wonder about the language, learn its features, and become word historians.

In *Spelling for Writers*, students will

- study words "from the inside out" and notice patterns.

- understand where words come from and why they are spelled the way they are.

- transfer knowledge of word patterns from their spelling lists to their writing.

- learn proofreading techniques that are applicable to all writing.

In *Spelling for Writers*, teachers will have

- easy-to-follow weekly lessons.

- an organized way to manage individualized word lists.

- built-in differentiated instruction.

- support from the Teacher's Edition, Transparencies, Posters, and CD-ROM.

- flexibility in deciding how the program best meets their students' needs.

Annotated Lesson

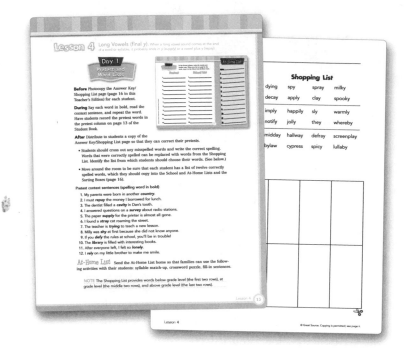

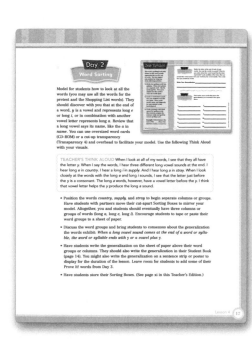

Day 1 includes a teacher-directed pretest. Students create their own word lists for study by replacing correctly spelled words with Shopping List words. This list offers students additional at-grade-level words or, for students needing differentiated instruction, words below or above grade level. Students copy the final list onto the School and At-Home Lists in the Student Book. The At-Home List tears out of the Student Book. On the back is the Dear Families letter that provides weekly communication with students' families.

Day 2 is hands-on and active. Teachers use the Teacher's Think Aloud and large word cards (from the CD-ROM), or a cut-up transparency (from the Transparencies) to model how to sort the words. Eventually, students take over the sorting themselves. Students collaboratively form a generalization that states what spelling pattern makes the words similar or different. The focus of word sorting is for students to compare and contrast words in order to observe dependable spelling features.

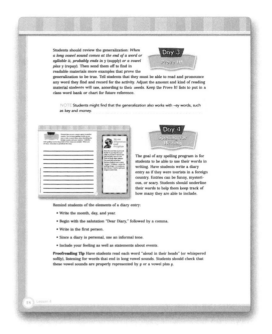

Days 3-4

Students find words in sources outside the program that prove the generalization. Discussion and sharing of the words expands students' word knowledge. As students become more aware of a particular feature, they begin to see it and hear it everywhere!

Students show what they know about the word feature in a writing assignment. Specific proofreading tips help students become more accurate writers.

The word history feature encourages a curiosity about language. Once students get hooked, they will want to know where every word came from!

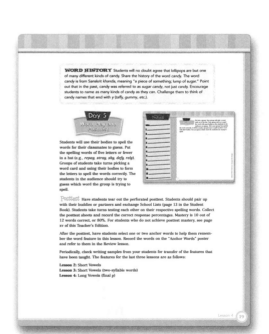

Day 5

The posttest shows whether students understand the word feature they have studied. The posttest tears out of the Student Book for convenience.

The word play activities are appropriate for independent, paired, or small group work. They can be used to bring the concept to closure or for review before the posttest.

5-Day Plan

Day of the Week	Purpose	What the teacher does	What the students do
Day 1 **Pretest and** **Word Lists** *15-20 minutes*	Assess current level of knowledge of word feature. Establish a word list for the week.	Orally presents words in context sentences. Hands out answer keys for students to self-correct their pretests. Circulates, providing guidance as students self-select words from the Shopping List.	Take pretest. Proofread own attempts. Highlight incorrect attempts. Select words from Shopping List to replace any correctly spelled words. Copy words onto the School List and At-Home List. Fill in Sorting Boxes. Take the At-Home List home!
Day 2 **Word Sorting** *15-20 minutes*	Identify common sound and spelling patterns and sort the words into groups with similar word features.	Prepares master set of Sorting Boxes. Use cards in pocket chart or an overhead to model sorting for the group. Brings group to consensus on generalization related to the word features. Records and displays the generalizations.	Cut apart Sorting Boxes. Sort words into categories that make sense. Write a generalization about the words in the Student Book. Share discoveries during whole-class discussion.

Day of the Week	Purpose	What the teacher does	What the students do
Day 3 **Prove It!** *5 minutes of initial instruction, independent search during other literacy work, 10 minutes to share words*	Prove the generalization and apply it to a larger of pool of words in the "real world."	Revisits generalization. Give direction for words search (i.e., where students will hunt for more words that are similar to the pattern). Discusses words that fit the pattern and those that do not.	Find words that are similar to this week's pattern. Students may work independently or collaboratively. Record words in the Student Book.
Day 4 **Spelling for Writing** *5 minutes of instruction, independent writing during other literacy work*	Write words in context and practice proofreading skills.	Assigns the writing assignment and teaches the proofreading tip.	Create written text in the Student Book using this week's words. Proofread writing.
Day 5 **Word Play** **and Posttest** *10 minutes*	Review words through word play. Assess knowledge of the feature.	Supervises posttest given by spelling buddies or administers posttest. Collects and grades the posttest. Looks for 80% mastery. Returns to generalization with students to select "anchor" words to use to remember the spelling feature.	Use Student Book for word play. Take the posttest.

Variation for 3-day plan:

Day 1 Pretest and Word Sort

Day 2 Prove It! and Spelling for Writing

Day 3 Word Play and Posttest

Classroom Management

Fitting Spelling for Writers into Literacy Instruction

Instructional settings and needs vary across classrooms. However, *Spelling for Writers* is flexible enough to use in any classroom setting.

Fitting Spelling for Writers into the Language Arts Class *Spelling for Writers* fits with other literacy instruction because a student's word knowledge is essential in all areas of literacy – reading, writing, listening, and speaking. *Spelling for Writers* offers teachers another opportunity to discuss how we can read and write words. The writing activity can easily be carried over to writing workshop, as many of the *Spelling for Writing* ideas are good "starters" that could be continued in workshop time. The Four Blocks® approach includes a word analysis component, and the sorting and word play days are compatible with the philosophy of that program. Word hunts and word histories could become a center.

Flexible Scheduling *Spelling for Writers* is set up as a five-day routine. Many teachers do their spelling lessons from Monday through Friday; however, the authors recommend starting on Tuesday or Wednesday and going into the next week so that families have the weekend to work on the activities in the Dear Families letter. The lessons can be adapted in the following ways:

- Combine activities to form a three-day routine (see page ix).
- The word hunt activity on Day 3 and the writing activity on Day 4 can be handled by the students once they have direction from the teacher. Therefore, they can be used any time during the literacy instruction, as homework assignments, or as on-going activities.
- Limit the time allotted for certain activities, such as the word hunt, writing, and word play.

Customizing the Lists

Day 1 includes a pretest that is teacher directed, followed by the students' involvement in creating a word list for study. How this list is developed can vary depending on the instructional needs. The intent is for students to self-select, but in particular classrooms or at particular times of the year, the teacher may choose to be more directive in influencing student lists. Whichever way the lists are developed, all students will be examining the same word feature.

Whole Class Use the pretest words for everyone and work only with those words throughout the cycle of activities, all the way through the teacher-administered posttest. For teachers new to the program, this is a good way to manage the lessons at the beginning of the year while they and the students become familiar with *Spelling for Writers* and each other. Once teachers and students are comfortable with the program, they can begin to incorporate elements of customization.

Small Groups Teachers who already manage several reading groups for literacy instruction can use those same groups for spelling instruction. Each group can work with the teacher to determine the word list for the lesson. At the end of the week, the teacher administers the posttest to each group.

Individuals *Spelling for Writers* will be most effective if each student has a customized list. Student motivation is a powerful learning tool, and when students feel ownership and in control of their words, they are motivated to learn. Teachers can advise students which section of the Shopping List to use (below, on, or above grade level), based on very specific knowledge of how students are doing in spelling or in accordance with the students' reading levels. Spelling buddies can use each other's School List to test each other. Teachers then collect and grade the posttests.

Managing the Word Cards

One of the challenges of word sorting is how to handle the sorting boxes, or word cards.

Making the Word Cards

- Photocopy the Answer Key/Shopping List page for students each week. When their lists are ready, have them copy the words into the boxes. This can be a homework assignment if students have filled in their At-Home List.
- Photocopy the copy master from the Transparencies and Copy Master folder for each student. Only the pretest words are on this sheet.
- Use the CD-ROM to produce word cards for students or large word cards to use when modeling a word sort for the class.

Using the Word Cards

- Once students have made their final sorts, they can preserve them by taping or gluing the word cards to a sheet of paper. Slip the paper inside the back cover of the Student Book for the week or keep all the sorts in a separate spelling folder.
- To keep the cards available for re-use, have students store the cards (see below).
- Word cards can be kept in a word study center for students to use in their free time. They can also be sent home for further practice.

Storing the Word Cards

- Store the cards in envelopes or resealable plastic bags. Label each envelope or bag with the lesson number. A class set of envelopes or bags can be stored in the *Spelling for Writers* box or in a file box in the word study center.
- Use a paper clip to keep the cards together. Attach the word cards to the inside back cover of the Student Book.
- Instead of storing the word cards, new word cards can be printed out as needed from the CD-ROM.

[Handwritten margin notes:]
How will we test the kids at the end of the week? 3 groups.
Use card stock!
Put cards in a baggie in writing folder.
Make spelling notebooks for each kid.
Keep extra bags on hand.

How the Words Were Chosen

Pretest Words

Using several research based word lists, the pretest words were selected from lists used by nearly every research-based spelling series. These include lists that analyzed the highly frequent reading and writing words for particular grade levels. The word lists in the early years begin with rime patterns, proven to be the highest occurring primary words in students' reading and writing. Lists used as a resource for this key component to the lessons were Dale and O'Rourke's *Living Word Vocabulary* (1976), Greene's *New Iowa Spelling Scale* (1961), Hanna, Hanna, Hodges and Rudorf's *Phoneme-grapheme Correspondences as Cues to Spelling Improvement* (1966), Henderson's *Teaching Spelling* (1990), Dolch's *High-Frequency Sight Words List* (1936), and Wylie and Durrell's *37 phonograms* (1970). Additionally, the linguistic research that focuses on the developmentally appropriate continuum for learning to spell guided the selection of the grade level features. The work of Read (1971), Henderson (1977, 1990), Templeton (1989), and Schlagal (1992) provided the match between grade levels and the features on which the lessons focus. Once the features and grade levels were matched, the researched lists were used to select grade level words that would serve as excellent models for the students to work with and observe the spelling features. At the primary grades, lists of 6-8 words were devised. At the upper elementary grades, lists of 12 words were created. These word lists provide the students opportunity to carefully examine patterns so that they get into how the patterns sound and are spelled. Only then can they generalize their new learning to other words they choose to write. These numbers are also manageable for the sorting day and to provide the teacher with manageable numbers for meeting individual needs.

Shopping List Words

Using the same careful selection as in the pretest words, additional words at each grade level were selected. Should individualization be needed, students can select from below- or above-grade-level words. This shows students the wide range of words using the same pattern. It also permits a community of learning to occur: All students are looking at the exact same pattern, even though they are using words appropriate to their reading and writing level.

Repetition of Words

Occasionally teachers may notice a word being used more than once in a school year for more than one feature. By examining a word in more than one way, we reinforce to students that it is about developing strategies for becoming a better speller—not about memorizing a word for the posttest. Often, the second time a student comes to a word, he or she will remember it in a different way. This provides another dependable resource for students: There are multiple ways to look at and remember the spellings of words.

Frequently Asked Questions

What is a word feature? A word feature is a spelling pattern that can be observed across a number of English words. The feature helps us both read and write a word. There are many dependable features of our language that we can help students learn to provide power to their reading and writing. For example, when we see English words that are Consonant, Vowel, Consonant (CVC), we know that the vowel has a short sound. This feature, then, is a short vowel sound.

What is a generalization? A generalization is a statement about the feature that a group of words share. *Spelling for Writers* selects the spelling features that have the broadest application in English words and will help develop dependable strategies for students when writing independently. Establishing the generalization of the spelling feature is a way for students to organize their thinking about words.

Why is word sorting important? Sorting is the hands-on, active learning element of *Spelling for Writers*. The sorting activity gives students a way "into" words. It provides a concrete, manipulative way to learn new words. Because they talk about, listen to, look at, and analyze words, students learn more about how to spell a large number of words.

Why can't students just memorize the words? A memorization model limits students to using only the correct spelling and usage of words they can remember. Research demonstrates that memorization can disempower some learners who need a variety of strategies available to them. Strategies that broaden a student's understanding of the language provide multiple opportunities for students to expand their knowledge

How is the instruction in *Spelling for Writers* differentiated? The philosophy of *Spelling for Writers* has been applied to a wide range of learners. Students study the same feature but have individualized lists because the Shopping List offers additional words below, at, and above grade level. Support is provided for every learner in the following ways: The teacher can adjust the number of words, the teacher or students can select the difficulty of words, and students can work with a knowledgeable peer.

How does *Spelling for Writers* work with English Learners? *Spelling for Writers* helps English Learners by helping them understand how English works. Memorizing words does not help these learners apply their knowledge outside the posttest. *Spelling for Writers* helps them see the patterns and discover ways to make connections across a large number of words. Pretest context sentences are provided to help students understand the words tested: conversations during the sorting and word play help students with their speaking and listening vocabulary.

Is it OK for students to give each other the posttest? The question of "cheating" sometimes comes up in the context of buddy situations. Since students understand the focus is on word features rather than whole words, the stigma of being a "master" of a certain number of words is removed. Instead, they are part of a community of learners working to master a spelling feature and its many applications in the English language.

Assessment in *Spelling for Writers*

Formal Weekly Tests

Pretest Each lesson begins with a teacher-directed pretest, given through context sentences. Students record the words in the Student Book. Teachers have the option of correcting the test themselves, but the power of *Spelling for Writers* lies in the empowerment of students and their ability to take control of their learning. Students check the words against the Answer Key. They copy the correct spelling of misspelled words from the Answer Key, and they replace correctly spelled words with Shopping List words.

The pretest is the starting point for studying a word feature. It shows what students know about the word feature, even though the feature is not "announced" at the time of the pretest. Students will be encouraged to discover it the next day. However, once they realize how the lists are organized, many students will begin to predict what the feature is as they take the pretest.

Posttest The purpose of the posttest is to see how well students have learned the word feature they studied during the week. If students have customized their lists, the posttest will show whether they can generalize the feature. The teacher can give the posttest to the whole class or to small groups, or spelling buddies can give the test to each other. Record posttest scores in the class record chart on Teacher's Edition page 180.

Periodic Developmental Assessment

Review Because *Spelling for Writers* focuses on helping students understand, learn, and apply the spelling features in English, the review weeks focus, once again, on the spelling features. Following each lesson's posttest, the teacher and students collaboratively establish a couple of anchor words and record them on the "Anchor Words" poster. These are the words that students can refer to when applying the knowledge learned during the lessons. When giving the pretest for the review weeks, teachers can once again observe how students are applying their knowledge. There are three ways the teacher may give this pretest:

- The teacher can announce the feature and ask the students to write a word that contains that features. ("Write a word that is a compound word.")

- The teacher can refer to the anchor word. ("When we studied compound words, we selected *wristwatch* as an anchor word to help us remember that feature. What is another compound word?")

- The teacher can give the students options of words she or he has chosen from the previous lessons. ("Which of these words is compound? Listen as I say three words— *Tuesday, wristwatch, happily*. Write the compound word.").

For any words students write correctly, they should be asked to go back to their word hunt for that week and find a word they would like to add to their list to learn

Use pre-test words for Anchor words.

to spell. Again, the teacher may choose words for the students to select from by looking back at the posttest, or selecting from the CD-ROM. This review week provides one more opportunity for the students to learn the feature and to understand they are not memorizing words; rather, they are learning how the English language works so that they develop dependable strategies for application to writing.

Benchmark Assessment *Spelling for Writers* provides assessment opportunities three times across every grade level. Specifically, these benchmark assessments allow the teacher to observe the features students already know that will be taught in the coming year. This will help with differentiated instruction for all types of learners. By repeating the assessment mid-year and end of the year, the teacher has concrete evidence of growth. This provides documentation to parents, schools, and other educators working with the students. Since the same words are used each time, the teacher can directly observe how the students' strategies are changing and improving.

Classroom Writing The real "test" of whether students understand the generalizations is in their writing. As students learn more word features, teachers should hold them accountable for using the features in their writing. At the end of every three lessons in *Spelling for Writers*, there is a reminder to the teacher to check students' writing for accurate use of recently learned word features.

Grading the Posttest and Reteaching

On the posttest, 10 correctly spelled words out of 12 is considered mastery of the feature. If students score below that level, try the reteaching activities listed below.

Number Correct	12	11	10	9	8	7	6	5	4	3	2	1
Percentage	100%	92%	83%	75%	66%	58%	50%	42%	33%	25%	17%	8%

Reteaching the Word Feature Students who do not understand the word feature can be helped with the following suggestions:

- Find out what the student was thinking when he or she made an attempt at writing a word. Ask questions such as the following:
  - What were you hearing and thinking about as you wrote this word?
  - What other words like this do you know?
  - How might you remember how this spelling pattern sounds and looks?
  - Let's try writing this again. You listen as I say it, then I want you to proofread what you wrote and see if you it looks like the word I said.

- Keep a set of word cards available. Have the student sort the words and explain the sort to you. Then, have the student do the sort repeatedly. Sorting speed is not competition between students; rather, an individual can do timed sorts to beat his or her own record. Speed sorting leads to automaticity, which in turn leads to more fluent reading and writing.

We reteach the features of the words.

Spelling for Writers Scope and Sequence

Word Feature	Grade 1	Grade 2	Grade 3	Grade 4	Grade 5	Grade 6
Vowels						
Short	x	x	x	x	x	x
In word families	x	x	x			
In closed syllable		x	x	x	x	x
In multisyllabic words		•	x	x	x	x
Long	x	x	x	x	x	x
/e/ marker	•	x	x	x		
Vowel sound of /y/		•	x	x	x	x
In silent letter patterns		•	x	x	x	x
R-controlled			•	x	x	x
More complex				•	x	x
Complex patterns			•	x	x	x
Diphthongs			•	x	x	x
Alternations				•	x	x
Consonants						
Alphabet	x					
Initial	x	x				
Final	x	x				
Final k, ck		•				
Within words	x	x				
Blends		x	x	x		
Digraphs		x	x		x	x
Preconsonant nasals		•		x	x	
Soft and hard sound of /c/ and /g/		•				
Patterns qu, ph, mb		•				
Silent patterns		•	x	x		x
Doubling before adding endings			•	x	x	
Doubling at syllable juncture				•		x
Alternations						•
Meaning Influences						
Prefixes			•	x	x	x
Absorbed/Assimilated					•	x
Greek/Latin					•	x
Numerical						•
Suffixes			•	x	x	x
Endings -tion, -sion, -cian					•	x
-ible, -able						•
-al, -el, -le						•
Plurals		•	x	x	x	x
Plural irregular forms			•	x	x	x
Past tense		•	x	x		
Past tense irregular forms		•	x	x		
Comparatives		•	x	x	x	x
Superlatives			•	x	x	x
Greek/Latin					•	x
Homonyms			•	x		
Derivations and relations				•	x	x
Compound words			•	x	x	x
Contractions				•	x	
Dictionary terms				•	x	x
Possessives					•	x
Words from other languages					•	
Synonyms/Antonyms					•	x
Homographs					•	
Greek/Latin roots					•	x
Eponyms					•	x
Portmanteau words					•	
Acronyms					•	
Idioms						•
Onomatopoeia						•

• introduction
x review

3x year

Days 1-2
Word Lists

2 days

Before Have students turn to page 1 in the Student Book, where they will record the spelling words.

During Say each word in boldface (page 2) aloud. The word features in parentheses are for your information only. These words were specifically chosen because they represent grade level words for that feature. If you substitute any other words, use those words in Lessons 20 and 36. It is recommended that this assessment be administered over two to five days, in short intervals, in order to best meet the needs of your students and to avoid student fatigue. On Days 3-5, if the assessment is still ongoing, students can continue with the other activities after you administer a small portion of the assessment.

After Interpret students' responses, analyzing first their successes in spelling a word that meets the word feature criterion and then taking a hard look at where they may have miscued, perhaps recalling a different word feature and misapplying it. We suggest you do not mark in the Student Book. A record sheet is provided (see page 179 in this Teacher's Edition). This records the features and allows you to document growth for each student. It is important for students not to see the markings, so simply transfer any attempts to the record sheet. This reinforces the understanding that *Spelling for Writers* developmentally supports the spelling strategies that students bring to their writing, rather than focusing on mastery of whole words. As you will notice, the students' profile easily documents growth.

Benchmark Assessment The Benchmark Assessment occurs in Lessons 1, 20, and 36 to measure students' growth and development in spelling across the year. The same words must be used each time in order to have a consistent way to measure students' growth on each feature.

Day 1

1. **acid** (short vowel)
2. **button** (short vowel in 2-syllable words)
3. **angry** (long vowels, final *y*)
4. **chase** (*e* marker)
5. **mule** (*e* marker)
6. **close** (*e* marker)
7. **dime** (*e* marker)
8. **Pete** (*e* marker)
9. **avenue** (long vowels, silent letter pattern)
10. **doubtful** (consonant, silent letter pattern)
11. **southerner** (*r*-controlled vowels)
12. **snowbound** (diphthong)
13. **studios** (plurals)
14. **done** (irregular past-tense)
15. **withhold** (compound words)
16. **wrapping** (doubling before ending or suffix)
17. **uncommon** (prefix)

Day 2

18. **painless** (suffix)
19. **angel/angelic** (derivations and relations)
20. **slammed** (blends)
21. **lovelier/loveliest** (comparatives)
22. **threw/through** (homonyms)
23. **taught** (complex vowel pattern)
24. **launch** (preconsonant nasals)
25. **knee/knelt** (vowel alternations)
26. **accurate** (doubling at syllable juncture)
27. **odor** (*r*-controlled in more complex words)
28. **incorrect** (prefixes and meanings)
29. **connect** (doubling at syllable juncture)
30. **undoable** (prefix/suffix in the same word)
31. **oxen** (irregular plurals)
32. **shoreline** (compound words)
33. **missed/mist** (homonyms)
34. **wouldn't** (contractions)

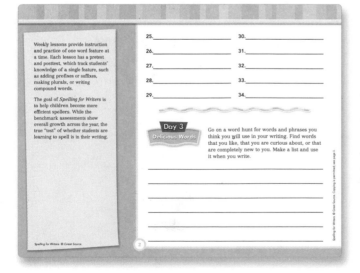

Letter to the Families

On pages 1–2 of the Student Book, there is a letter addressed to your students' families. The letter explains in a brief way the purpose of benchmark assessments: examining the student's responses enables you to measure the student's knowledge of word features studied this year, a prerequisite for expanding the student's spelling strategies. Please take time to read the letter. It will help you understand that benchmark assessments are your opportunity to examine how children are progressing.

Day 3
Delicious Words

If students are still taking the benchmark assessment, administer more of the words before students begin the word-hunt activity. *(day 3)*

Pique students' interest in words by sending them on a word hunt for "delicious" words that they can use to enhance their writing. The words can be single or in phrases, completely unknown words, or words students would like to learn more about. When students find words that interest them, they take ownership of the words.

Model what you mean by "delicious" words by sharing some words or phrases that attract your attention or catch your ear. When you read a book aloud, point out the "delicious" words that the author used. For example, in *The Great Kapok Tree* author Lynne Cherry uses these phrases: "the beat and the hum of the forest had lulled him to sleep," "a troupe of monkeys scampered down from the canopy," and "because his coat blended into the dappled light and shadows." In *The Talking Eggs,* retold by Robert San Souci, there are examples of figurative language such as "sharp as forty crickets" and "alike as two peas in a pod."

Have students share with the class some of the words they found. Guide the class to select words to be recorded on the "Delicious Words" poster. Students can use the poster as a resource of terrific words to use in their writing.

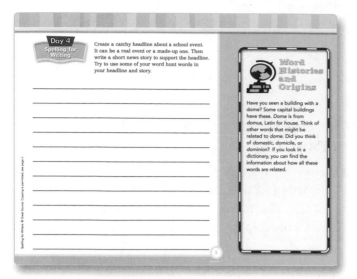

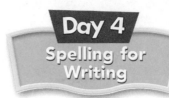

Day 4
Spelling for Writing

Tie this prompt in with H-Mifflin book.

The goal of any spelling program is for students to be able to use accurate spelling to convey a message. Encourage students to use some of the words from the word hunt to write a newspaper headline about a real or imagined event at their school. Then, students can write a news story that supports the headline. Offer students these tips about writing a headline and news story:

• A headline is catchy and usually short—just long enough to catch the reader's attention and tell the reader what the news story is about.

• A news story answers the questions *Who? What? Where? When? Why?* and sometimes *How?*

Proofreading Tip Reading and proofreading are very different. When students read, their eyes sweep over the text and their brains are processing the author's message. When students proofread, their eyes should slow down to focus on each individual word. Suggest that students touch a pencil point to each word as they proofread.

Proofreading T.

Word History The word *dome* comes from the Latin word *domus*, which means "house." Originally, it referred only to stately homes. It also means "lord and master." On page 4, students are asked to find other words that could mean house. Examples: *hut, shack, castle, apartment, barracks, dormitory,* and *cabin.*

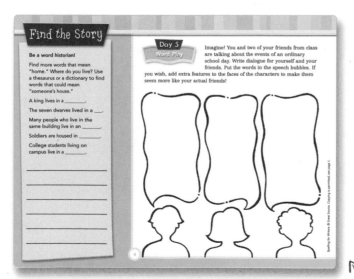

Day 5
Word Play

Your students have been asked to write dialogue about an ordinary school day. They must imagine that they are talking with two friends. Students write their dialogue in speech bubbles. You may wish to have groups of students read their dialogues aloud.

Use quotation marks

Teach dialogue during narrative writing.

Lesson 2 Short Vowels.
Every word in English has at least one of the vowels. These words have short vowel sounds: *drag, kept, grip, odd,* and *luck.*

Day 1
Pretest and Word Lists

Before Photocopy the Answer Key/ Shopping List page (page 6 in this Teacher's Edition) for each student.

During Say each word in bold, read the context sentence, and repeat the word. Have students record the pretest words in the pretest column on page 5 of the Student Book.

After Distribute to students a copy of the Answer Key/Shopping List page so that they can correct their pretests.

- Students should cross out any misspelled words and write the correct spelling. Words that were correctly spelled can be replaced with words from the Shopping List. Identify the list from which students should choose their words. (See below.)

- Be sure that each student has a list of twelve correctly spelled words, which they should copy into the School and At-Home Lists and the Sorting Boxes (page 6).

Pretest context sentences (spelling word in bold)

1. The wrestler had a strong **grip** when I shook his hand.
2. Mom will **knit** me a sweater.
3. I **kept** my baseball card collection in a box.
4. Three is an **odd** number, but four is even.
5. The lightning **struck** the tree during the storm.
6. The **ditch** in the yard is full of mud.
7. I **brush** my cat's fur to keep it from tangling.
8. California is on the **west** coast of the United States.
9. We go to the **dock** to see ships arrive.
10. John sharpens the **dull** pencil point.
11. I **drag** my heavy bag because it is too heavy to carry.
12. Alex must **practice** the violin when she gets home.

At-Home List
Send the At-Home List home so that families can use the following activities with their children: short vowel fill-ins, riddles, silly sentences, and word count.

NOTE The Shopping List provides words below grade level (the first two rows), at grade level (the middle two rows), and above grade level (the last two rows).

Name _____

Answer Key

1. grip
2. knit
3. kept
4. odd
5. struck
6. ditch
7. brush
8. west
9. dock
10. dull
11. drag
12. practice

Shopping List

just	luck	olive	problem
list	gift	cent	send

press	cash	lump	kick
inch	scrub	plum	sob

absent	asset	dromedary	bunch
candid	octopus	crisp	ugly

Sorting Boxes

Word Sorting

Model for students how to look at all the words (you may use all the words for the pretest and the Shopping List words). They should discover with you that every word in English has at least one vowel; all the words in this lesson have a short vowel sound that is represented by *a, e, i, o,* or *u.* You may wish to review the vowels and their respective short sounds with students. You can use oversized word cards (CD-ROM) or a cut-up transparency (Transparency 2) and overhead to facilitate your model. Use the following Think Aloud with your visuals.

[handwritten, right margin:] From other books or as homework.

[handwritten, left margin:] he feature is the vowel sound.

> **TEACHER'S THINK ALOUD** What do I notice about my words? I know that every word in English must have at least one vowel sound, so I will think about sorting my words by their vowel sounds. When I say the words, I hear that they have short vowel sounds. I will say each word to myself and decide which short vowel sound I hear. Then I will look for the letter that represents the sound and underline it. For example, the word *grip* has the short *i* vowel sound. I will underline the letter *i.* The word *kept* has the short *e* sound. I will underline the letter *e.*

[handwritten, left margin:] Model on overhead screen. →

- Position the words *grip* and *kept* to begin two separate columns or groups. Have students with partners move their cut-apart Sorting Boxes to mirror your model. Altogether, you and students should eventually have five columns or groups of words (short *a,* short *e,* short *i,* short *o,* short *u*).

- Encourage students to tape or paste their word groups to a sheet of paper. Some words may fit two columns. For example, *practice* may be entered in the short *a* or short *i* column.

- Discuss the word groups and bring students to consensus about the generalization the words exhibit: *Every word in English has at least one vowel; all the words in this lesson have a short vowel sound that is represented by* a, e, i, o, *or* u.

- Have students write the generalization on the sheet of paper above their word groups or columns. They also write the generalization in their Student Book (page 6). You may also write the generalization on a sentence strip or poster to display for the week. Be sure to leave room for students to add some of their Prove It! words.

- Have students take the Posttest. (See page xi in this Teacher's Edition.)

*[handwritten note, overlaid:] * Post test. Split class up by two levels take one group from middle list the other group from the top list.*

[Inset image — Student Book page and "Dear Families," letter:]

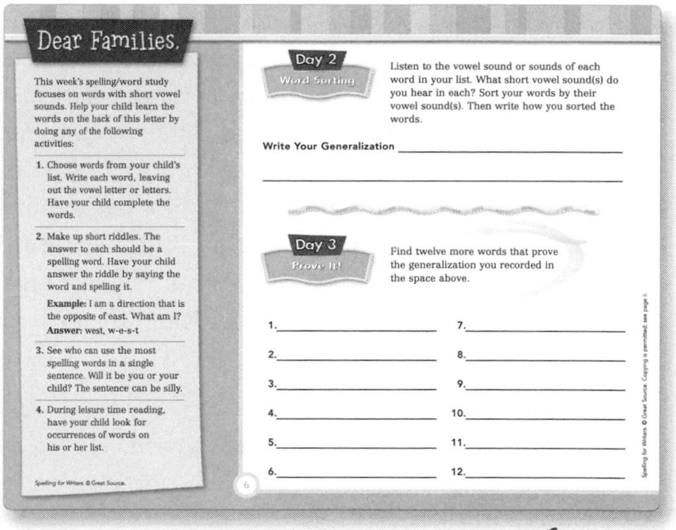

Dear Families,

This week's spelling/word study focuses on words with short vowel sounds. Help your child learn the words on the back of this letter by doing any of the following activities:

1. Choose words from your child's list. Write each word, leaving out the vowel letter or letters. Have your child complete the words.

2. Make up short riddles. The answer to each should be a spelling word. Have your child answer the riddle by saying the word and spelling it.
   Example: I am a direction that is the opposite of east. What am I?
   Answer: west, w-e-s-t

3. See who can use the most spelling words in a single sentence. Will it be you or your child? The sentence can be silly.

4. During leisure time reading, have your child look for occurrences of words on his or her list.

Day 2 Word Sorting — Listen to the vowel sound or sounds of each word in your list. What short vowel sound(s) do you hear in each? Sort your words by their vowel sound(s). Then write how you sorted the words.

Write Your Generalization _____

Day 3 Prove It! — Find twelve more words that prove the generalization you recorded in the space above.

1._____ 7._____
2._____ 8._____
3._____ 9._____
4._____ 10._____
5._____ 11._____
6._____ 12._____

Students should review the generalization: *Every word in English has at least one vowel; all the words have a short vowel sound that is represented by* a, e, i, o, *or* u. Then send them off to find in readable materials more examples that prove the generalization to be true. Tell students that they must be able to read and pronounce any word they find and record for the activity. Adjust the amount and kind of reading material students will use and the number of words students should find, according to their needs. Keep the Prove It! lists to put in a class word bank or chart for future reference.

Day 3
Prove It!

NOTE Suggest that students look in a math book for words such as *add, subtract, number, solve, problem,* and *division.*

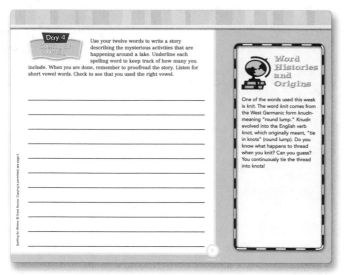

Day 4
Spelling for Writing

The goal of any spelling program is for students to be able to use their words in writing. Have students write a story about recent mysterious activities that happen at a lake. The focus of this activity is for students to demonstrate knowledge of their spelling words, but remind students of the elements of a good story:

• A story should have a beginning, middle, and end.

• The story should have a setting, or time and place, and characters.

Proofreading Tip Explain that proofreading is not like regular reading. Proofreading should be done slowly and carefully. Have students touch each word with a finger or a pencil point to slow their reading.

WORD HISTORY Having learned about the word *knit*, students might be interested to know about the word *weave*. Explain that it comes from the Germanic *weben*. Ask volunteers what word they see in *weben*. Students should notice the word *web*. Describe the weaving process to students. Explain that when a person weaves, he or she is actually making a "web" of thread in order to make the cloth.

Give students clues that describe the twelve words from the pretest. Specify to students that the clues might be a synonym, a descriptive phrase, or an example. Students should write the answers on Student Book page 8.

Lesson 2
Posttest

name _____

1. _____
2. _____
3. _____
4. _____
5. _____
6. _____
7. _____
8. _____
9. _____
10. _____
11. _____
12. _____

Day 5
Word Play

Listen to the clues your teacher says. These clues describe this week's spelling words. The clues might be synonyms, descriptive phrases, or examples. Can you guess what word is being described? Write your answers on the numbered lines.

1. _____
2. _____
3. _____
4. _____
5. _____
6. _____
7. _____
8. _____
9. _____
10. _____
11. _____
12. _____

Clues	Answers
1. rehearse	1. practice
2. how to make a sweater	2. knit
3. haul	3. drag
4. boring	4. dull
5. pier	5. dock
6. not even	6. odd
7. firm handshake	7. grip
8. where the sun sets	8. west
9. stored	9. kept
10. paint and hair are two types	10. brush
11. channel dug for drainage	11. ditch
12. hit	12. struck

Posttest Have students tear out the perforated posttest. Students should pair up with their buddies or partners and exchange School Lists (page 5 in the Student Book). Students take turns testing each other on their respective spelling words. Collect the posttest sheets and record the correct response percentages. Mastery is 10 out of 12 words correct, or 80%. For students who do not achieve posttest mastery, see page xv in this Teacher's Edition.

After the posttest, have students select one or two anchor words to help them remember the word feature in this lesson. Record the words on the "Anchor Words" poster and refer to them in the Review lesson.

Lesson 3

Short Vowels (two-syllable words). The words in this lesson all have at least one short vowel phoneme. Examples are *access*, *export*, and *drizzle*.

Before Photocopy the Answer Key/ Shopping List page (page 11 in this Teacher's Edition) for each student.

During Say each word in bold, read the context sentence, and repeat the word. Have students record the pretest words in the pretest column on page 9 of the Student Book.

After Distribute to students a copy of the Answer Key/Shopping List page so that they can correct their pretests.

- Students should cross out any misspelled words and write the correct spelling. Words that were correctly spelled can be replaced with words from the Shopping List. Identify the list from which students should choose their words. (See below.)

- Move around the room to be sure that each student has a list of twelve correctly spelled words, which they should copy into the School and At-Home Lists and the Sorting Boxes (page 11).

Pretest context sentences (spelling word in bold)

1. Only employees have **access** to the kitchen.
2. Oranges are an important **export** of Florida.
3. The adventurers will **explore** the new land.
4. Although there is just a light **drizzle**, I still need my umbrella.
5. What **aspect** of the math problem did you not understand?
6. The **clever** mouse never fell for the trap.
7. Buzzing mosquitoes **bother** me!
8. The flying **comet** glowed in the night sky.
9. The **usher** led us to our seats at the concert.
10. The **critic** hated the movie.
11. My dad will play **golf** on Saturday.
12. The posters of the **missing** child were posted everywhere.

At-Home List Send the At-Home List home so that families can use the following activities with their students: word scramble, riddles, oral story, and word count.

NOTE The Shopping List provides words below grade level (the first two rows), at grade level (the middle two rows), and above grade level (the last two rows).

Name _____

Answer Key

1. access
2. export
3. explore
4. drizzle
5. aspect
6. clever
7. bother
8. comet
9. usher
10. critic
11. golf
12. missing

Shopping List

| import | acid | estate | insect |
| plot | angle | robin | chill |

| dusk | glitter | puppy | inspect |
| visible | truck | shiver | swung |

| picnic | eggplant | snuggle | activity |
| ultra | exit | wring | ember |

Sorting Boxes

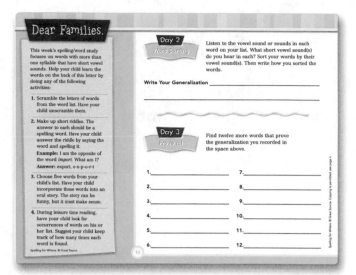

Model for students how to look at all the words (you may use all the words for the pretest and the Shopping List words). They should discover with you that every word in English has at least one vowel; all the words in this lesson have a short vowel sound that is represented by *a, e, i, o,* or *u*. You may wish to review the vowels and their respective short sounds with students. You can use oversized word cards (CD-ROM) or a cut-up transparency (Transparency 3) and overhead to facilitate your model. Use the following Think Aloud with your visuals.

> **TEACHER'S THINK ALOUD** What do I notice about the words? When I say them aloud, I hear that each one has at least one short vowel sound. I will say each word to myself and decide what short vowel sound or sounds I hear. Then I will look for the letter that represents the sound and underline it. For example, the word *critic* has two short *i* vowel sounds. I will underline the letter *i* twice. The word *golf* has the short *o* sound. I will underline the letter *o*.

- Position the words *critic* and *golf* to begin two separate columns or groups. Have students with partners move their cut-apart Sorting Boxes to mirror your model. Altogether, you and students should eventually have five columns or groups of words (short *a,* short *e,* short *i,* short *o,* short *u*). Some words fit in two columns because they have two vowels. For example, *access* may be entered in the short *a* or short *e* column. Encourage students to tape or paste their word groups to a sheet of paper.

- Discuss the word groups and bring students to consensus about the generalization the words exhibit: *Every word in English has at least one vowel; all the words in this lesson have a short vowel sound that is represented by* a, e, i, o, *or* u.

- Have students write the generalization on the sheet of paper above their word groups or columns. They should also write the generalization in their Student Book (page 10). You might also write the generalization on a sentence strip or poster to display for the duration of the lesson. Leave room for students to add some of their Prove It! words from Day 3.

- Have students store their Sorting Boxes. (See page xi in this Teacher's Edition.)

Day 3
Prove It!

Students should review the generalization: *Every word in English has at least one vowel; all the words for this week have a short vowel sound that is represented by* a, e, i, o, *or* u. Then send them off to find in readable materials more examples that prove the generalization to be true. Tell students that they must be able to read and pronounce any word they find and record for the activity. Adjust the amount and kind of reading material students will use and the number of words students should find, according to their needs. To expose each student to more words, ask students to share their lists aloud with a partner or the class. Keep the Prove It! lists to put in a class word bank or chart for future reference.

Day 4
Spelling for Writing

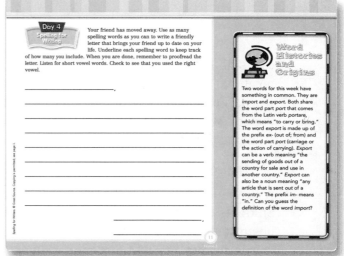

The goal of any spelling program is for students to be able to use their words in writing. Have students write a friendly letter to someone who has moved away. The letter should bring the friend up to date on the student's life. Students should underline their words to help them keep track of how many they are able to include.

To prepare students to write, talk together about topics that could be included in the letter, such as sports, music, friends, and school.

Remind students of the elements of a friendly letter:

- The letter should include a greeting, body, closing, and signature.
- The tone should be informal.
- Punctuation should be accurate.

Proofreading Tip Remind students to use a finger or pencil point to touch each word. They should listen for short vowel words and check to see that they used the right letter.

WORD HISTORY Relate the English word *port* to the Latin noun *portus,* "a door or gateway." Long ago, ships had a door on the left side to give access to a dock. That is why even today the left side of a ship is called the port side. The right side of a ship is called the starboard side. The term *starboard* comes from the Old English word *steor-bord,* meaning "steering side." Early ships had their steering oars on the right side. This also helped as they pulled up to the port.

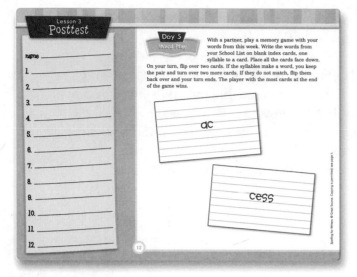

Have partners play a memory game with their words. Have students write their words on cards, one syllable to a card. (Make two cards for one-syllable words.) Students can refer to a dictionary for the syllables. For example, a student with the word *bother* writes *both* on one card and *er* on another. Students take turns flipping over two cards to see if they match to form a spelling word. If the cards do not match, the student flips the cards back over and puts them in the same position. Then it's the partner's turn. If the cards do match up and form a spelling word, the student takes possession of the two cards. The student with the most cards at the end wins. Keep sets of cards in a word study center or other accessible place for students to use in their spare time.

Posttest Have students tear out the perforated posttest. Students should pair up with their buddies or partners and exchange School Lists (page 9 in the Student Book). Students take turns testing each other on their respective spelling words. Collect the posttest sheets and record the correct response percentages. Mastery is 10 out of 12 words correct, or 80%. For students who do not achieve posttest mastery, see page xv in this Teacher's Edition.

After the posttest, have students select one or two anchor words to help them remember the word feature in this lesson. Record the words on the "Anchor Words" poster and refer to them in the Review lesson.

Lesson 4 Long Vowels (final *y*). When a long vowel sound comes at the end of a word or syllable, it probably ends in *y* (*supply*) or a vowel plus *y* (*repay*).

Day 1
Pretest and Word Lists

Before Photocopy the Answer Key/ Shopping List page (page 16 in this Teacher's Edition) for each student.

During Say each word in bold, read the context sentence, and repeat the word. Have students record the pretest words in the pretest column on page 13 of the Student Book.

Day 1 Word Lists In the Pretest column, write the words your teacher says. When your list is ready for the week, copy it in the School and At-Home Lists.

Pretest
1.
2.
3.
4.
5.
6.
7.
8.
9.
10.
11.
12.

School List
1.
2.
3.
4.
5.
6.
7.
8.
9.
10.
11.
12.

Lesson 4
At-Home List
name
1.
2.
3.
4.
5.
6.
7.
8.
9.
10.
11.
12.

After Distribute to students a copy of the Answer Key/Shopping List page so that they can correct their pretests.

- Students should cross out any misspelled words and write the correct spelling. Words that were correctly spelled can be replaced with words from the Shopping List. Identify the list from which students should choose their words. (See below.)

- Move around the room to be sure that each student has a list of twelve correctly spelled words, which they should copy into the School and At-Home Lists and the Sorting Boxes (page 16).

Pretest context sentences (spelling word in bold)

1. My parents were born in another **country**.
2. I must **repay** the money I borrowed for lunch.
3. The dentist filled a **cavity** in Dan's tooth.
4. I answered questions on a **survey** about radio stations.
5. The paper **supply** for the printer is almost all gone.
6. I found a **stray** cat roaming the street.
7. The teacher is **trying** to teach a new lesson.
8. Milly was **shy** at first because she did not know anyone.
9. If you **defy** the rules at school, you'll be in trouble!
10. The **library** is filled with interesting books.
11. After everyone left, I felt so **lonely**.
12. I **rely** on my little brother to make me smile.

At-Home List   Send the At-Home List home so that families can use the following activities with their students: syllable match-up, crossword puzzle, fill-in sentences.

NOTE The Shopping List provides words below grade level (the first two rows), at grade level (the middle two rows), and above grade level (the last two rows).

Name _____

Answer Key

1. country	7. trying
2. repay	8. shy
3. cavity	9. defy
4. survey	10. library
5. supply	11. lonely
6. stray	12. rely

Shopping List

dying	spy	spray	milky
decay	apply	clay	spooky
imply	happily	sly	warmly
notify	jolly	they	whereby
midday	hallway	defray	screenplay
bylaw	cypress	spicy	lullaby

Sorting Boxes

Day 2
Word Sorting

Model for students how to look at all the words (you may use all the words for the pretest and the Shopping List words). They should discover with you that at the end of a word, *y* is a vowel and represents long *e* or long *i*, or in combination with another vowel letter represents long *a*. Review that a long vowel says its name, like the *a* in *name*. You can use oversized word cards (CD-ROM) or a cut-up transparency (Transparency 4) and overhead to facilitate your model. Use the following Think Aloud with your visuals.

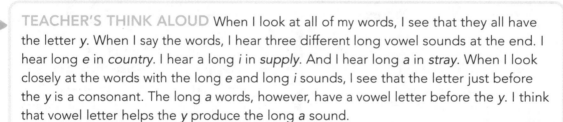

TEACHER'S THINK ALOUD When I look at all of my words, I see that they all have the letter *y*. When I say the words, I hear three different long vowel sounds at the end. I hear long *e* in *country*. I hear a long *i* in *supply*. And I hear long *a* in *stray*. When I look closely at the words with the long *e* and long *i* sounds, I see that the letter just before the *y* is a consonant. The long *a* words, however, have a vowel letter before the *y*. I think that vowel letter helps the *y* produce the long *a* sound.

- Position the words *country*, *supply*, and *stray* to begin separate columns or groups. Have students with partners move their cut-apart Sorting Boxes to mirror your model. Altogether, you and students should eventually have three columns or groups of words (long *a*, long *e*, long *i*). Encourage students to tape or paste their word groups to a sheet of paper.

- Discuss the word groups and bring students to consensus about the generalization the words exhibit: *When a long vowel sound comes at the end of a word or syllable, the word or syllable ends with* y *or a vowel plus* y.

- Have students write the generalization on the sheet of paper above their word groups or columns. They should also write the generalization in their Student Book (page 14). You might also write the generalization on a sentence strip or poster to display for the duration of the lesson. Leave room for students to add some of their Prove It! words from Day 3.

- Have students store their Sorting Boxes. (See page xi in this Teacher's Edition.)

Students should review the generalization: *When a long vowel sound comes at the end of a word or syllable, it probably ends in* y (supply) *or a vowel plus* y (repay). Then send them off to find in readable materials more examples that prove the generalization to be true. Tell students that they must be able to read and pronounce any word they find and record for the activity. Adjust the amount and kind of reading material students will use, according to their needs. Keep the Prove It! lists to put in a class word bank or chart for future reference.

NOTE Students might find that the generalization also works with –ey words, such as *key* and *money*.

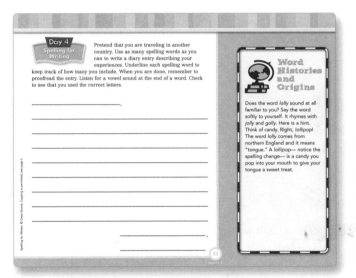

The goal of any spelling program is for students to be able to use their words in writing. Have students write a diary entry as if they were tourists in a foreign country. Entries can be funny, mysterious, or scary. Students should underline their words to help them keep track of how many they are able to include.

Remind students of the elements of a diary entry:

- Write the month, day, and year.

- Begin with the salutation "Dear Diary," followed by a comma.

- Write in the first person.

- Since a diary is personal, use an informal tone.

- Include your feeling as well as statements about events.

Proofreading Tip Have students read each word "aloud in their heads" (or whispered softly), listening for words that end in long vowel sounds. Students should check that these vowel sounds are properly represented by *y* or a vowel plus *y*.

WORD HISTORY Students will no doubt agree that lollipops are but one of many different kinds of candy. Share the history of the word *candy*. The word *candy* is from Sanskrit *khanda*, meaning "a piece of something; lump of sugar." Point out that in the past, candy was referred to as *sugar candy*, not just candy. Encourage students to name as many kinds of candy as they can. Challenge them to think of candy names that end with *y* (*taffy, gummy,* etc.).

Day 5
Word Play and Posttest

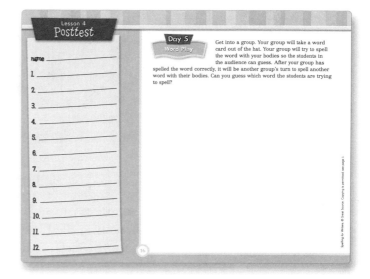

Students will use their bodies to spell the words for their classmates to guess. Put the spelling words of five letters or fewer in a hat (e.g., *repay, stray, shy, defy, rely*). Groups of students take turns picking a word card and using their bodies to form the letters to spell the words correctly. The students in the audience should try to guess which word the group is trying to spell.

Posttest Have students tear out the perforated posttest. Students should pair up with their buddies or partners and exchange School Lists (page 13 in the Student Book). Students take turns testing each other on their respective spelling words. Collect the posttest sheets and record the correct response percentages. Mastery is 10 out of 12 words correct, or 80%. For students who do not achieve posttest mastery, see page xv of this Teacher's Edition.

After the posttest, have students select one or two anchor words to help them remember the word feature in this lesson. Record the words on the "Anchor Words" poster and refer to them in the Review lesson.

Periodically, check writing samples from your students for transfer of the features that have been taught. The features for the last three lessons are as follows:

Lesson 2: Short Vowels
Lesson 3: Short Vowels (two-syllable words)
Lesson 4: Long Vowels (final *y*)

Lesson 5

Long Vowels (e marker). When a word ends with a silent *e*, the vowel closest to the silent *e* represents a long vowel sound. Examples are *fade*, *shine*, and *globe*.

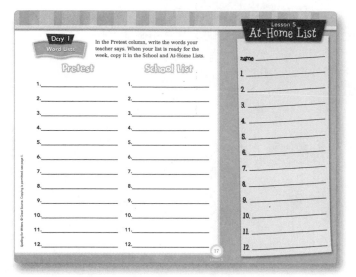

Day 1
Pretest and Word Lists

Before Photocopy the Answer Key/Shopping List page (page 21 in this Teacher's Edition) for each student.

During Say each word in bold, read the context sentence, and repeat the word. Have students record the pretest words in the pretest column on page 17 of the Student Book.

After Distribute to students a copy of the Answer Key/Shopping List page so that they can correct their pretests.

- Students should cross out any misspelled words and write the correct spelling. Words that were correctly spelled can be replaced with words from the Shopping List. Identify the list from which students should choose their words. (See below.)

- Move around the room to be sure that each student has a list of twelve correctly spelled words, which they should copy into the School and At-Home Lists and the Sorting Boxes (page 21).

Pretest context sentences (spelling word in bold)

1. The answer was an **absolute** NO!
2. The wax really made the car **shine**.
3. Can you find Africa on the **globe**?
4. Jane's **perfume** smells like roses.
5. It was so cold that Mike **chose** not to go outside.
6. His **pride** was hurt after losing two games in a row.
7. When the pond **froze** over, we went skating.
8. He **spoke** so fast that no one understood him.
9. She won first prize, not once, but **twice**!
10. Crocodiles and alligators are **alike** in many ways.
11. Colorful shirts can **fade** after too much washing.
12. The marathon was a twenty-six-**mile** run.

At-Home List
Send the At-Home List home so that families can use the following activities with their students: word scramble/unscramble, spelling word sentences, word with same spelling pattern, and definitions.

NOTE The Shopping List provides words below grade level (the first two rows), at grade level (the middle two rows), and above grade level (the last two rows).

Name _____

Answer Key

1. absolute	7. froze
2. shine	8. spoke
3. globe	9. twice
4. perfume	10. alike
5. chose	11. fade
6. pride	12. mile

Shopping List

trade	knife	price	stone
huge	slope	skate	June
broke	stripe	locate	grove
tube	spine	theme	concrete
revoke	strike	mute	envelope
fume	code	scribe	refuse

Sorting Boxes

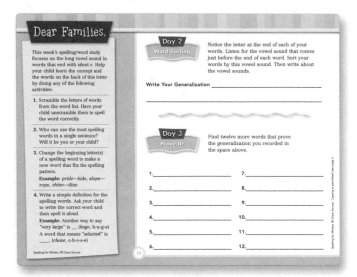

Model for students how to look at all the words (you may use all the words for the pretest and the Shopping List words). They should discover with you that when a word ends with silent *e*, the vowel that is closest to the silent *e* represents a long vowel sound. You can use oversized word cards (CD-ROM) or a cut-up transparency (Transparency 5) and overhead to facilitate your model. Use the following Think Aloud with your visuals.

TEACHER'S THINK ALOUD When I look at the words, I immediately notice that all of them end with the letter *e*. Then I read the words to myself and notice that the final *e* is silent. When I reread the words carefully, I figure out that the vowel closest to the silent *e* represents a long vowel sound. I will say each word to myself and decide what long vowel sound I hear. For example, in the word *shine* I hear a long *i* sound. In *perfume* I hear a long *u* sound in the second syllable. I will continue to look for more long vowel sounds to make more columns for my word sort.

• Position your words to begin two separate columns or groups. Have students with partners move their cut-apart Sorting Boxes to mirror your model. Altogether, you and students should eventually have five columns or groups of words (long *a*, long *e*, long *i*, long *o*, long *u*). Encourage students to tape or paste their word groups to a sheet of paper.

• Discuss the word groups and bring students to consensus about the generalization the words exhibit: *When a word ends with silent* e, *the vowel that is closest to the silent* e *makes a long vowel sound*.

• Remind students to use this information when they proofread their writing. If a word has a long vowel sound, students should ask themselves whether the word should end in *e*.

• Have students write the generalization on the sheet of paper above their word groups or columns. They should also write the generalization in their Student Book (page 18). You might also write the generalization on a sentence strip or poster to display for the duration of the lesson. Leave room for students to add some of their Prove It! words from Day 3.

• Have students store their Sorting Boxes. (See page xi in this Teacher's Edition.)

Day 3
Prove It!

Students should review the generalization: *When a word ends with silent* e, *the vowel that is closest to the silent* e *represents a long vowel sound.* Then send them off to find in readable materials more examples that prove the generalization to be true. Tell students that they must be able to read and pronounce any word they find and record for the activity. Adjust the amount and kind of reading material students will use and the number of words students should find, according to their needs. To expose each student to more words, ask students to share their lists aloud with a partner or the class. Keep the Prove It! lists to put in a class word bank or chart for future reference.

NOTE Students may find words, such as *have* or *come*, that do not fit the generalization. Set these words aside in a separate category. (See Word History on Teacher's Edition page 24.)

Day 4
Spelling for Writing

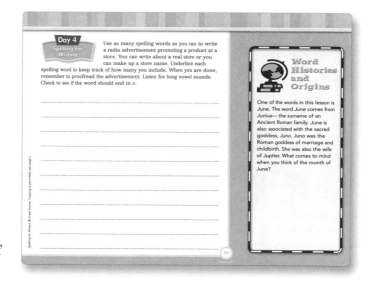

The goal of any spelling program is for students to be able to use their words in writing. Have students write a radio advertisement promoting a product in a store of their choosing. Students may choose to write about a real store, or they can make one up. Students should underline their words to help them keep track of how many they are able to include.

Remind students of the elements of an effective radio advertisement:

• The purpose of an advertisement is to persuade.

• Use superlatives; words such as the "Super Blowout Sale" imply "super" savings and "mega" bargains to customers.

• Use emotionally charged language and words with positive connotations to encourage customers to buy your product.

• The tone should be energetic.

• Punctuation should convey the writer's emotions.

Proofreading Tip Have students read each word "aloud in their heads" (or whispered softly), listening for words that have long vowel sound. Students should decide whether these words should be spelled with the *e* marker.

WORD HISTORY The silent *e*-marker works so beautifully for *snake* and *bike*. But why do we have words like *come* and *love*? The English language hit a period in time when no words ended in *u* or *v*. It has been documented that *e* was simply added to these words for visual purposes, not marking purposes as in *snake*. This was primarily a function of the scribes. In the case of *love*, the scribes did not like the way it looked with *u* and *v* together. First, *u* was changed to *o*. Then *e* was added. Through all of that, the pronunciation remained the same. Remember, too, that the tools for writing were calligraphy pens. Sometimes, the ink bled, closing *u* to become *o*. The next person who copied the word probably read the letter as an *o*. So, it was *cum* or *com*, then *come* with no pronunciation change.

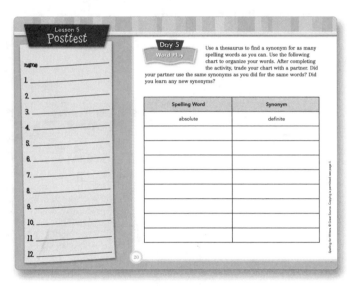

Day 5

Word Play and Posttest

Have available several copies of a thesaurus for students to use or access an online thesaurus. Demonstrate how to look up a word to find a synonym. Have students find a synonym for as many words as they can. After students complete the activity, encourage them to find a partner and compare charts. Have students trade lists to see who found more synonyms for his or her words. Then they can look for spelling words that are common to both lists and notice whether the synonyms they found are the same or different! (Sample answers: *shine-glow, chose-selected, spoke-talked, alike-similar, fade-diminish*)

Posttest Have students tear out the perforated posttest. Students should pair up with their buddies or partners and exchange School Lists (page 17 in Student Book). Students take turns testing each other on their respective spelling words. Collect the posttest sheets and record the correct response percentages. Mastery is 10 out of 12 words correct, or 80%. For students who do not achieve posttest mastery, see page xv in this Teacher's Edition.

After the posttest, have students select one or two anchor words to help them remember the word feature in this lesson. Record the words on the "Anchor Words" poster and refer to them in the Review lesson.

Lesson 6 Long Vowels (silent letter patterns). Sometimes vowel letters make a pattern in which one vowel is long and one is silent, as in *beast, float, paint,* and *elbow.*

Day 1
Pretest and Word Lists

Day 1
Word Lists

In the Pretest column, write the words your teacher says. When your list is ready for the week, copy it in the School and At-Home Lists.

Pretest

School List

Lesson 6
At-Home List

name _____

Before Photocopy the Answer Key/ Shopping List page (page 26 in this Teacher's Edition) for each student.

During Say each word in bold, read the context sentence, and repeat the word. Have students record the pretest words in the pretest column on page 21 of the Student Book.

After Distribute to students a copy of the Answer Key/Shopping List page so that they can correct their pretests.

- Students should cross out any misspelled words and write the correct spelling. Words that were correctly spelled can be replaced with words from the Shopping List. Identify the list from which students should choose their words. (See below.)

- Move around the room to be sure that each student has a list of twelve correctly spelled words, which they should copy into the School and At-Home Lists and the Sorting Boxes (page 26).

Pretest context sentences (spelling word in bold)

1. A Tyrannosaurus rex is an example of a huge **beast**.
2. A feather will **float** on water.
3. As he got sleepy, his **dreamy** eyes were beginning to close.
4. My clothes got **soaked** when I got caught in a rainstorm.
5. A human **brain** is more complex than a computer.
6. A person who is lazy is referred to as a **loafer**.
7. A **follower** must respect his or her leader.
8. Mark must **clean** the mess he made in the kitchen.
9. The art teacher is helping us learn to **paint**.
10. I hurt my **elbow** when the door banged my arm.
11. Since the lawn **mower** is broken, I cannot cut the grass.
12. The magician wears a top hat and a black **cloak**.

At-Home List Send the At-Home List home so that families can use the following activities with their students: word clues, word count, smaller words.

NOTE The Shopping List provides words below grade level (the first two rows), at grade level (the middle two rows), and above grade level (the last two rows).

Name _____

Answer Key

1. beast
2. float
3. dreamy
4. soaked
5. brain
6. loafer
7. follower
8. clean
9. paint
10. elbow
11. mower
12. cloak

Shopping List

narrow	yellow	tail	raining
peach	afraid	either	beacon
oatmeal	painful	dainty	eagle
entertainment	growth	tease	season
bleacher	seacoast	league	tomorrow
stagecoach	moonbeam	waist	sneak

Sorting Boxes

Day 2
Word Sorting

Model for students how to look at all the words (you may use all the words for the pretest and the Shopping List words). They should discover with you that sometimes two side-by-side vowel letters make a pattern in which one vowel represents a long vowel sound while the other vowel is silent. You can use oversized word cards (CD-ROM) or a cut-up transparency (Transparency 6) and overhead to facilitate your model. Use the following Think Aloud with your visuals.

Day 2 Word Sorting Look for two vowels together in each word. Remember that sometimes *w* can be a vowel. Listen for the one sound the two letters represent together. Sort your words by their vowel sounds. Then write about the vowel sounds.

Write Your Generalization _____

_____

Day 3 Prove It! Find twelve more words that prove the generalization you recorded in the space above.

1._____   7._____
2._____   8._____
3._____   9._____
4._____   10._____
5._____   11._____
6._____   12._____

> **TEACHER'S THINK ALOUD** All of the words have something in common. I see two vowel letters next to each other in each word. When I say each word, though, I hear only one vowel sound. It is the long vowel sound I associate with the first of the two vowel letters. For example, the word *clean* has the long *e* vowel sound. The word *paint* has the long *a* sound. The second letter in each vowel pair must be silent.

- Position your words to begin two separate columns or groups. Have students with partners move their cut-apart Sorting Boxes to mirror your model. Altogether, you and students should eventually have three columns or groups of words (long *a*, long *e*, long *o*). Encourage students to tape or paste their word groups to a sheet of paper.

- Discuss the word groups and bring students to consensus about the generalization the words exhibit: *Sometimes two side-by-side vowel letters make a pattern in which one vowel represents a long vowel sound while the other vowel is silent.*

- Demonstrate how this generalization works by comparing these words: *best/beast, float/flat,* and *pant/paint.* Remind students to include both vowels when they write these and similiar long vowel words.

- Have students write the generalization on the sheet of paper above their word groups or columns. They should also write the generalization in their Student Book (page 22). You might also write the generalization on a sentence strip or poster to display for the duration of the lesson. Leave room for students to add some of their Prove It! words from Day 3.

- Have students store their Sorting Boxes. (See page xi in this Teacher's Edition.)

Students should review the generalization: *Sometimes two side-by-side vowel letters make a pattern in which one vowel represents a long vowel sound while the other vowel is silent.* Then send them off to find in readable materials more examples that prove the generalization to be true. Tell students that they must be able to read and pronounce any word they find and record for the activity. Adjust the amount and kind of reading material students will use and the number of words students should find, according to their needs. To expose each student to more words, ask students to share their lists aloud with a partner or the class. Keep the Prove It! lists to put in a class word bank or chart for future reference.

NOTE Students may find words, such as *head* or *town*, that look like they follow the generalization but do not. Set these aside in a separate category.

Day 3
Prove It!

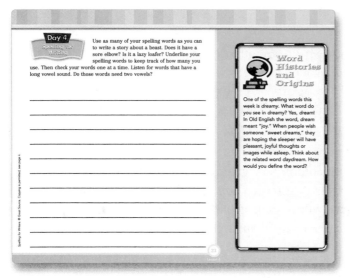

Day 4
Spelling for Writing

Have students use as many of their spelling words as possible to write a story about a beast. Although the purpose of the story is for students to demonstrate their use of the spelling words, offer them these tips for writing a story:

• Focus on one major event.

• Establish a setting (time and place).

• Develop the character(s) through their actions and dialogue.

Proofreading Tip Remind students that proofreading is different from regular reading. It is slower and more methodical. Have them read aloud "in their heads" or whisper the words so that they hear each one, listening specifically for long vowel sounds and checking to see if two vowels are needed.

WORD HISTORY Pose the question: if a *dream* is a pleasant, joyful sleep experience, what is the opposite? As students respond, write the word *nightmare*. Ask for informal definitions. Then explain that *mare* comes from the Old English *moere*, which is an evil spirit or goblin that supposedly sat on sleepers' chests and produced a feeling of suffocation. Originally, when people spoke of a *nightmare*, they were referring to this evil spirit. The definition changed to "a horrible or terrifying dream, fear, or experience" after the sixteenth century.

Using the dollar amounts in the chart below, have students figure out how much five of their words are worth. After students figure out the value of the five words (they can use calculators), they should calculate their grand total. Encourage students to compare their list's value to a partner's. Which student is the richest?

A = $1	B = $2	C = $3	D = $4	E = $5	F = $6	G = $7
H = $8	I = $9	J = $10	K = $11	L = $12	M = $13	N = $14
O = $15	P = $16	Q = $17	R = $18	S = $19	T = $20	U = $21
V = $22	W = $23	X = $24	Y = $25	Z = $26		

Pretest words

1. beast = $47
2. float = $54
3. dreamy = $66
4. soaked = $55
5. brain = $44
6. loafer = $57
7. follower = $106
8. clean = $35
9. paint = $60
10. elbow = $57
11. mower = $74
12. cloak = $42

Total = $697

Posttest Have students tear out the perforated posttest. Students should pair up with their buddies or partners and exchange School Lists (page 21 in the Student Book). Students take turns testing each other on their respective spelling words. Collect the posttest sheets and record the correct response percentages. Mastery is 10 out of 12 words correct, or 80%. For students who do not achieve posttest mastery, see page xv in this Teacher's Edition After the posttest, have students select one or two anchor words to help them remember the word feature in this lesson. Record the words on the "Anchor Words" poster and refer to them in the Review lesson.

Lesson 7 Silent Consonant Patterns.

Consonant letters can make a pattern in which one is silent, for example *tomb*, *knife*, and *gnaw*.

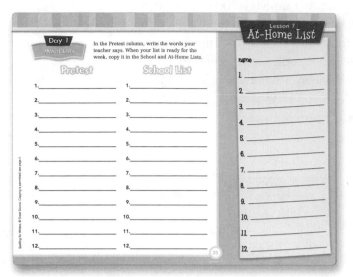

Day 1
Pretest and Word Lists

Before Photocopy the Answer Key/Shopping List page (page 31 in this Teacher's Edition) for each student.

During Say each word in bold, read the context sentence, and repeat the word. Have students record the pretest words in the pretest column on page 25 of the Student Book.

After Distribute to students a copy of the Answer Key/Shopping List page so that they can correct their pretests.

- Students should cross out any misspelled words and write the correct spelling. Words that were correctly spelled can be replaced with words from the Shopping List. Identify the list from which students should choose their words. (See below.)

- Move around the room to be sure that each student has a list of twelve correctly spelled words, which they should copy into the School and At-Home Lists and the Sorting Boxes (page 31).

Pretest context sentences (spelling word in bold)

1. Many of my ancestors are buried in a large **tomb**.
2. I need to **comb** my hair before I have my picture taken.
3. My dad has a real **knack** for building with wood.
4. You need to slice the bread with a **knife**.
5. I have no **doubt** that I will pass the test.
6. It is difficult to try to grab a cup without using your **thumb**.
7. The **knight** rode in on his white horse to save the princess.
8. The tiny **gnat** was bothering me as it flew in front of my face.
9. You will need to turn the **knob** to open the door.
10. Dad needs to **align** the wheels of the car for a smooth ride.
11. The dog will **gnaw** on its new bone.
12. The bill reminded Jason of his **debt**.

At-Home List Send the At-Home List home so that families can use the following activities with their students: categories and word count.

NOTE The Shopping List provides words below grade level (the first two rows), at grade level (the middle two rows), and above grade level (the last two rows).

Name _____

Answer Key

1. tomb	7. knight
2. comb	8. gnat
3. knack	9. knob
4. knife	10. align
5. doubt	11. gnaw
6. thumb	12. debt

Shopping List

knock	knew	limb	gnu
sign	lamb	knee	crumb
kneel	plumber	knead	subtle
climb	gnarl	knothole	knoll
knuckle	foreign	plumbing	gnome
design	knowledge	knapsack	cologne

Sorting Boxes

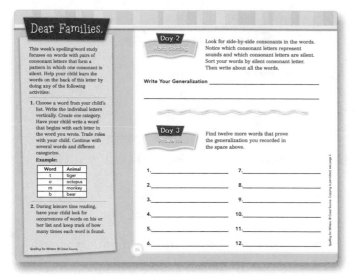

Model for students how to look at all the words (you may use all the words for the pretest and the Shopping List words). They should discover with you that sometimes pairs of consonant letters form a pattern in which one consonant is silent. You can use oversized word cards (CD-ROM) or a cut-up transparency (Transparency 7) and overhead to facilitate your model. Use the following Think Aloud with your visuals.

TEACHER'S THINK ALOUD When I pronounce the words, I notice that not every consonant is sounded. For example, when I examine *comb*, I see two consonant letters, *m* and *b*, at the end, yet I hear only the sound *m* represents. That means the consonant *b* must be silent. The case with *knife* is similar. In the consonant pair *kn*, I hear only the sound *n* represents. The *k* is silent. I will sort all the words by their silent consonant.

- Position your words to begin two separate columns or groups. Have students with partners move their cut-apart Sorting Boxes to mirror your model. Altogether, you and students should eventually have three columns or groups of words (silent *b*, silent *k*, silent *g*). Encourage students to tape or paste their word groups to a sheet of paper.

- Discuss the word groups and bring students to consensus about the generalization the words exhibit: *Sometimes pairs of consonant letters form a pattern in which one consonant is silent.*

- Have students write the generalization on the sheet of paper above their word groups or columns. They should also write the generalization in their Student Book (page 26). You might also write the generalization on a sentence strip or poster to display for the duration of the lesson. Leave room for students to add some of their Prove It! words from Day 3.

- Have students store their Sorting Boxes. (See page xi in this Teacher's Edition.)

Students should review the generalization: *Sometimes pairs of consonant letters form a pattern in which one consonant is silent.* Then send them off to find in readable materials more examples that prove the generalization to be true. Tell students that they must be able to read and pronounce any word they find and record for the activity. Adjust the amount and kind of reading material students will use and the number of words students should find, according to their needs. To expose each student to more words, ask students to share their lists aloud with a partner or the class. Keep the Prove It! lists to put in a class word bank or chart for future reference.

The goal of any spelling program is for students to be able to use their words in writing. Have students write an action-adventure story map. Discuss some popular adventure story lines to help get their ideas going. (Examples: *Spy Kids* and *Harry Potter*) Students should underline their words to help them keep track of how many they are able to include.

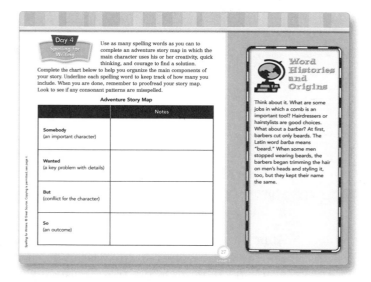

Share these tips with students:

- Reread what you have written to see if it makes sense and follows the directions for the activity.

- Look for any word omissions. (Sometimes the brain gets ahead of the hand!)

- Tally the number of spelling list words included; can you add more?

Proofreading Tip Tell students to touch each word with a finger or pencil point, looking especially for words that have silent-consonant patterns and checking to see that both consonants are there. Students will need to rely on their "spelling eye" to notice when silent consonants are missing.

WORD HISTORY Students may be interested to know that *comb* is an ancient word, which has been traced back to Indo-European *gombhos*, meaning "tooth"; Sanskrit *jambhas*, meaning "tooth"; and Greek *gophos*, meaning "pin" or "tooth." Ask students why or how the word *comb* is related to teeth. Explain that *comb* can be both a verb and a noun. Read this sentence and ask students to tell the meaning of *comb*: The police will *comb* the woods for traces of evidence. Share the meaning: *comb* can mean "to search thoroughly."

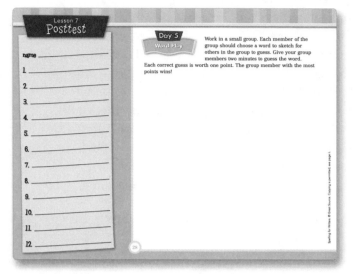

Day 5
Word Play and Posttest

Put all the word cards for this week in a hat. Group the students into several small teams. A student from each team picks a word card from the hat and tries to draw what the word represents for his or her teammates. The team has two minutes to guess the correct word. Each correct guess is worth one point. The team with the most points after all the words have been drawn wins the game.

Posttest Have students tear out the perforated posttest. Students should pair up with their buddies or partners and exchange School Lists (page 25 in Student Book). Students take turns testing each other on their respective spelling words. Collect the posttest sheets and record the correct response percentages. Mastery is 10 out of 12 words correct, or 80%. For students who do not achieve posttest mastery, see page xv in this Teacher's Edition.

After the posttest, have students select one or two anchor words to help them remember the word feature in this lesson. Record the words on the "Anchor Words" poster and refer to them in the Review lesson.

Periodically, check writing samples from your students for transfer of the features that have been taught. The features for the last three lessons are as follows:

Lesson 5: Long Vowels (*e* marker)
Lesson 6: Long Vowels (silent letter patterns)
Lesson 7: Silent Consonant Patterns

Lesson 8 R-Controlled Vowels.
When *r* follows a vowel, the *r* influences, or controls, the vowel sound. Examples are *pillar*, *germs*, *thirty*, and *motor*.

Day 1
Pretest and Word Lists

Before Photocopy the Answer Key/ Shopping List page (page 36 in this Teacher's Edition) for each student.

During Say each word in bold, read the context sentence, and repeat the word. Have students record the pretest words in the pretest column on page 29 of the Student Book.

After Distribute to students a copy of the Answer Key/Shopping List page so that they can correct their pretests.

- Students should cross out any misspelled words and write the correct spelling. Words that were correctly spelled can be replaced with words from the Shopping List. Identify the list from which students should choose their words. (See below.)

- Be sure that each student has a list of twelve correctly spelled words, which they should copy into the School and At-Home Lists and the Sorting Boxes (page 36).

Pretest context sentences (spelling word in bold)

1. A car has a powerful **motor**.
2. Flies **bother** me in the summer.
3. A **pillar** at each corner of the porch holds up the roof.
4. The **actor** plays a detective in his latest movie.
5. The comedy show was **crazier** than I expected.
6. The librarian set up a reading area in a **corner** of the room.
7. How long would it take to travel around the **world**?
8. My dad drinks his coffee with milk and **sugar**.
9. A **beggar** is someone who asks others for money or goods.
10. A quarter and a nickel add up to **thirty** cents.
11. Dirty sponges contain many **germs**.
12. My **sister** is the only girl in the family.

At-Home List Send the At-Home List home so that families can use the following activities with their students: guessing game, word search.

NOTE The Shopping List provides words below grade level (the first two rows), at grade level (the middle two rows), and above grade level (the last two rows).

Name _____

Answer Key

1. motor
2. bother
3. pillar
4. actor
5. crazier
6. corner
7. world
8. sugar
9. beggar
10. thirty
11. germs
12. sister

Shopping List

March	flirted	circle	spark
worm	other	shirt	harm
barber	clerk	circus	forty
party	orange	charge	chirp
porch	hermit	circuit	orchard
giraffe	garbage	fjord	numerator

Sorting Boxes

Day 2
Word Sorting

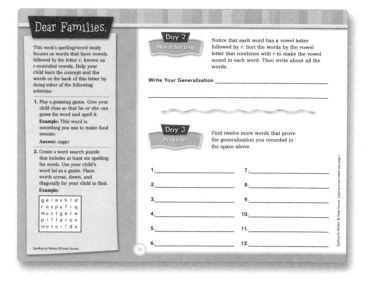

Model for students how to look at all the words (you may use all the words for the pretest and the Shopping List words). They should discover with you that when a vowel is followed by the letter *r*, the *r* influences (or controls) the sound of the vowel. You can use oversized word cards (CD-ROM) or a cut-up transparency (Transparency 8) and overhead to facilitate your model. Use the following Think Aloud with your visuals.

TEACHER'S THINK ALOUD When I look at my words, I see that they have something in common. All the words have a vowel right before the letter *r*. When I pronounce the words, I can hear that the sound of the *r* slightly changes the sound of the vowel before it. For example, when I say *corner*, I don't hear a short *o* or a long *o* vowel sound. When I say *thirty*, I don't hear either a short or long *i* sound.

- Position the two example words to begin two separate columns or groups (*o+r*, *i+r*). Have students with partners move their cut-apart Sorting Boxes to mirror your model. Altogether, you and students should eventually have four columns or groups of words (*a+r*, *e+r*, *i+r*, *o+r*). Encourage students to tape or paste their word groups to a sheet of paper.

- Discuss the word groups and bring students to consensus about the generalization the words exhibit: *When a vowel is followed by the letter* r, *the* r *influences (or controls) the sound of the vowel.*

- All the pretest words have the same *r*-controlled vowel sound (/ər/) but the sound is represented by different vowel letters plus *r*. Students will have to develop a "spelling eye" to remember that *beggar*, for example, ends with *-ar*, and *corner* ends with *-er*.

- Have students write the generalization on the sheet of paper above their word groups or columns. They should also write the generalization in their Student Book (page 30). You might also write the generalization on a sentence strip or poster to display for the duration of the lesson. Leave room for students to add some of their Prove It! words from Day 3.

- Have students store their Sorting Boxes. (See page xi in this Teacher's Edition.)

Students should review the generalization: *When a vowel is followed by the letter* r, *the* r *influences (or controls) the sound of the vowel.* Then send them off to find in readable materials more examples that prove the generalization to be true.

Tell students that they must be able to read and pronounce any word they find and record for the activity. Adjust the amount and kind of reading material students will use or the number of words students should find, according to their needs. To expose each student to more words, ask students to share their lists aloud with a partner or the class. Keep the Prove It! lists to put in a class word bank or chart for future reference.

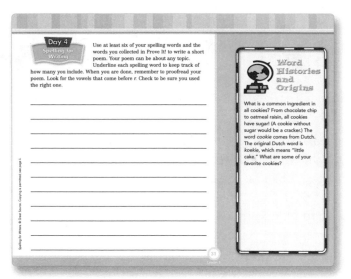

Day 4
Spelling for Writing

The goal of any spelling program is for students to be able to use their words in writing. Have students write a poem using at least six of their spelling words. Students should underline their words to help them keep track of how many they are able to include.

Remind students that poems

- are written in lines and stanzas (groups of lines),

- say a lot in a few words,

- often are very descriptive,

- sometimes have rhythm and/or rhyme, and

- may use repeated words as a special effect.

Proofreading Tip Have students find each word that has an *r* and underline it. Then remind students to use their "spelling eyes" to see whether they used the correct vowel in the words that have *r*-controlled vowels.

WORD _____ sugar they think goes into
the mix for _____ pound cake _____ they think goes into a
_____ moist, plain cake in a loaf
form.) Expla _____ ooking practices. In the
old times, r _____ he ingredients were listed
as a "poun _____ mean that in the old days,
a cake was _____ at's a lot of sugar!
Today's pou _____

Day 5
Word Play and Posttest

Have students play a memory game with
their words. Have students find a partner.
Each student writes his or her words on
cards, one word to a card. Then students
turn all twenty-four cards face down and
arrange them in four columns of six cards
each. Students take turns flipping over two
cards to see if they can match the *r*-con-
trolled vowels. If the cards do not have
words with the same *r*-controlled vowels,
the student flips the cards back over and puts them in the same position. Then it's
the partner's turn. If the cards do have the same *r*-controlled vowels, the student takes
possession of the two cards. The student with the most cards at the end wins.

Posttest Have students tear out the perforated posttest. Students should pair up
with their buddies or partners and exchange School Lists (page 29 in Student Book).
Students take turns testing each other on their respective spelling words. Collect the
posttest sheets and record the correct response percentages. Mastery is 10 out of 12
words correct, or 80%. For students who do not achieve posttest mastery, see page xv
in this Teacher's Edition.

After the posttest, have students select one or two anchor words to help them remember the word feature in this lesson. Record the words on the "Anchor Words" poster
and refer to them in the Review lesson.

Posttest

name _____
1. _____
2. _____
3. _____
4. _____
5. _____
6. _____
7. _____
8. _____
9. _____
10. _____
11. _____
12. _____

Day 5
Word Play

Get a partner. You and your partner write your
spelling words on cards— one word to a card.
Turn all twenty-four cards face down and
arrange them in four rows of six cards each.
Each partner takes a turn selecting two cards. If the two cards have
words with the same *r*-controlled vowels (like the cards below), the
partner gets to keep the pair of cards and goes again. If the cards do
not have words with the same *r*-controlled vowels, turn the cards back
over so your partner can play. Continue until all pairs have been made.
The partner with the most cards at the end of the game wins!

actor

motor

Lesson 9 Diphthongs. Two side-by-side vowels can represent a sound that is neither short nor long. Examples are *moist*, *gown*, *loyal*, and *pound*.

Day 1
Pretest and Word Lists

Before Photocopy the Answer Key/ Shopping List page (page 41 in this Teacher's Edition) for each student.

During Say each word in bold, read the context sentence, and repeat the word. Have students record the pretest words in the pretest column on page 33 of the Student Book.

After Distribute to students a copy of the Answer Key/Shopping List page so that they can correct their pretests.

- Students should cross out any misspelled words and write the correct spelling. Words that were correctly spelled can be replaced with words from the Shopping List. Identify the list from which students should choose their words. (See below.)

- Be sure that each student has a list of twelve correctly spelled words, which they should copy into the School and At-Home Lists and the Sorting Boxes (page 41).

Pretest context sentences (spelling word in bold)

1. You should use a *moist* sponge to clean up the spill.
2. The bride wore a sparkly, white wedding *gown*.
3. The rubber ball will *bounce* off the floor.
4. *Noise* is not allowed in the library.
5. I need to go to the deli for a *pound* of cheese.
6. Legend says that wolves *howl* at the full moon.
7. The cowboy will *mount* the horse.
8. When I hurt my knee I yelled, *ouch*!
9. We just bought a new *couch* for the living room.
10. When you feel sad, you *frown*.
11. After I brush my teeth, my *mouth* feels clean.
12. I like the *clown* with the big red nose and the green wig.

At-Home List Send the At-Home List home so that families can use the following activities with their students: word chain, rhyming words, word crosses.

NOTE The Shopping List provides words below grade level (the first two rows), at grade level (the middle two rows), and above grade level (the last two rows).

Name _____

Answer Key

1. moist	7. mount
2. gown	8. ouch
3. bounce	9. couch
4. noise	10. frown
5. pound	11. mouth
6. howl	12. clown

Shopping List

coin	loud	sound	cloud
town	foil	down	boil
shout	doubt	decoy	loyal
powder	scout	point	blouse
envoy	turmoil	sirloin	lounge
stout	oyster	poise	cauliflower

Sorting Boxes

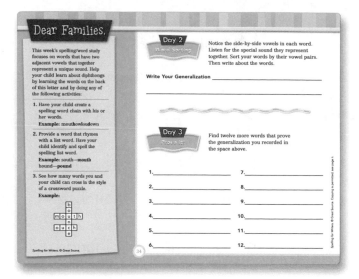

Day 2
Word Sorting

Model for students how to look at all the words (you may use all the words for the pretest and the Shopping List words). They should discover with you that a diphthong, or two vowels together, can represent a sound that is neither long nor short. You can use oversized word cards (CD-ROM) or a cut-up transparency (Transparency 9) and overhead to facilitate your model. Use the following Think Aloud with your visuals.

TEACHER'S THINK ALOUD When I look at my words, I see that they have something in common. All my words have two vowels right next to each other. (Remember, *w* is sometimes a vowel.) When I pronounce the words, I don't hear a long vowel sound or a short vowel sound for the two letters. I hear a sound that is kind of like a combination of both vowels—almost as if they are run together. I will try to sort my words by the vowel letters that are side by side. For example, in *moist*, *o* and *i* are side by side. In *mount*, *o* and *u* are together. My first two sorting groups are words with *oi* and words with *ou*.

- Position the cards for *moist* and *mount* to begin two separate columns or groups. Have students with partners move their cut-apart Sorting Boxes to mirror your model. Altogether, you and students should eventually have four columns or groups of words (*oi, ou, ow, oy*). (Students who are using just the pretest words will not have *oy* words.) Encourage students to tape or paste their word groups to a sheet of paper.

- Discuss the word groups and bring students to consensus about the generalization the words exhibit: *A diphthong, or two vowels together, can represent a sound that is neither long nor short.*

- Explain to students that when they write a word that has the /ou/ sound, they will have to rely on their "spelling eye," or visual memory, to know whether to use *ou* or *ow*.

- Have students write the generalization on the sheet of paper above their word groups or columns. They should also write the generalization in their Student Book (page 34). You might also write the generalization on a sentence strip or poster to display for the duration of the lesson. Leave room for students to add some of their Prove It! words from Day 3.

- Have students store their Sorting Boxes. (See page xi in this Teacher's Edition.)

Day 3

Prove It!

Students should review the generalization for this week's words: *A diphthong, or two vowels together, can represent a sound that is neither long nor short.* Then send them off to find in readable materials more examples that prove the generalization to be true. Tell students that they must be able to read and pronounce any word they find and record for the activity. Adjust the amount and kind of reading material students will use, according to their needs. To expose each student to more words, ask students to share their lists aloud with a partner or the class. Keep the Prove It! lists to put in a class word bank or chart for future reference.

NOTE Students may find words, such as *bowl, cough,* or *cougar,* that look like they follow the generalization but do not. Set these aside in a separate category.

Day 4

Spelling for Writing

The goal of any spelling program is for students to be able to use their words in writing. Have students group their School List words and Prove It! words into categories and write a label for each. Sample category ideas include number of syllables, part of speech, or meaning. Each category should have at least three words.

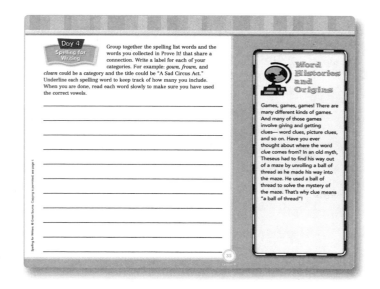

Proofreading Tip Students should touch each letter with a pencil point as they compare what they wrote against the printed Answer Key/Shopping List page (Teacher's Edition page 41). Another way to check for accuracy is to have students work in pairs: one student spells the word aloud, while the other checks each letter.

WORD HISTORY Relate the word *clue* to the familiar game of charades. Ask students who have played the game to describe how it works. Response should include that participants act out clues to words or syllables within words. Explain that *charades* comes from the French word *charrad,* for "conversation," and *charra,* for "chatter." Note that original clues in the game charades were written, not acted out.

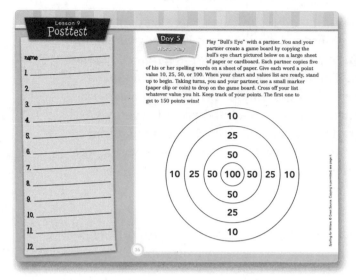

Have students play a game of "Bull's Eye" with their words. Have students find a partner and together copy the game board onto a large sheet of paper or cardboard. The center ring is worth 100 points. The second ring is worth 50 points. The third ring is worth 25 points. The outermost ring is worth 10 points. Have students choose five of their spelling words and assign values (10, 25, 50, 100) for each on a separate sheet of paper. Students then drop a marker (paper clip or coin) onto the game board to see where it lands. Each student checks off whatever value word the marker hits and scores that number of points. The first student to reach 150 points wins!

Posttest Have students tear out the perforated posttest. Students should pair up with their buddies or partners and exchange School Lists (page 33 in Student Book). Students take turns testing each other on their respective spelling words. Collect the posttest sheets and record the correct response percentages. Mastery is 10 out of 12 words correct, or 80%. For students who do not achieve posttest mastery, see page xv in this Teacher's Edition.

After the posttest, have students select one or two anchor words to help them remember the word feature in this lesson. Record the words on the "Anchor Words" poster and refer to them in the Review lesson.

Lesson 10 Plurals (-s, -es, y to i). Add -s to form the plural of most words (*rockets*). Add -es to words that end with *ch, x, s,* or *sh* (*arches*). Change *y* to *i* before *-es* (*berries*).

Day 1
Pretest and Word Lists

Before Photocopy the Answer Key/ Shopping List page (page 46 in this Teacher's Edition) for each student.

During Say each word in bold, read the context sentence, and repeat the word. Have students record the pretest words in the pretest column on page 37 of the Student Book.

After Distribute to students a copy of the Answer Key/Shopping List page so that they can correct their pretests.

- Students should cross out any misspelled words and write the correct spelling. Words that were correctly spelled can be replaced with words from the Shopping List. Identify the list from which students should choose their words. (See below.)

- Be sure that each student has a list of twelve correctly spelled words, which they should copy into the School and At-Home Lists and the Sorting Boxes (page 46).

Pretest context sentences (spelling word in bold)

1. The **rockets** will launch into space at noon.
2. You have to pass huge **arches** to enter the mansion.
3. Small white **crosses** marked the graves of the soldiers.
4. We will learn about **angles** in math class.
5. What do they manufacture in those **factories**?
6. I cannot see without my **glasses**.
7. The wind caused the **branches** to break off the tree.
8. The ball rolled behind the **bushes** in the park.
9. The **insects** flew around our picnic lunch.
10. Canvas and denim are **cloths** made from cotton.
11. My parents work for different **companies**.
12. The birds ate all the red **berries** off the bush.

At-Home List Send the At-Home List home so that families can use the following activities with their students: make words, plural words.

NOTE The Shopping List provides words below grade level (the first two rows), at grade level (the middle two rows), and above grade level (the last two rows).

Name _____

Answer Key

1. rockets
2. arches
3. crosses
4. angles
5. factories
6. glasses
7. branches
8. bushes
9. insects
10. cloths
11. companies
12. berries

Shopping List

horses	boxes	ladies	removes
babies	rises	hooks	kitties
stories	peaches	cities	axes
hobbies	segments	customs	loves
splashes	blushes	balloons	cameras
leashes	corners	marshes	strawberries

Sorting Boxes

Day 2
Word Sorting

At this point, students should begin to take more control of the sorting. Have students look at the words carefully and decide for themselves a way or ways in which they can sort the words (do an open sort.) Once they have made their sorts, have them write a generalization about the words. How students think about the words shows you what they understand about them.

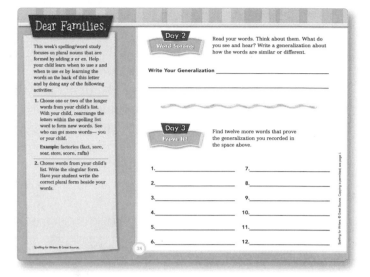

- If students have not reached consensus on their own, bring the class together to come to a consensus. Be certain to elicit ideas from the students that draw them to a common conclusion. You can use oversized word cards (CD-ROM) or a cut-up transparency (Transparency 10) and overhead to facilitate your model.

- Model for students a way to sort, using all the words. The two general categories for the sorting should be plural nouns that end with *s* and plural nouns that end with *-es*.

- Ask students to look carefully at the words in the *-es* group. Guide them to notice features of words that form the plurals with *-es*.

- Help students identify the singular base word for each plural. Then note how each word ends: with *sh*, *ch*, *x*, *ss*, or *y* preceded by a consonant letter.

- Model for students how to make a statement about how all their words were sorted: *Add* -s *to most words to form the plural, but add* -es *to words that end with* sh, ch, ss, x, *or* y *with a consonant before it*.

- Remind students that when *y* follows a consonant, it changes to *i* before *-es* is added (*berries*, but *keys*).

- Have students write the generalization in their Student Book (page 38). You might also write the generalization on a sentence strip or poster to display for the duration of the lesson. Leave room for students to add some of their Prove It! words from Day 3.

- Have students store their Sorting Boxes. (See page xi in this Teacher's Edition.)

Students should review the generalization: *All the words are plurals that are formed by adding -s or -es to a noun.* Then send them off to find in readable materials more examples that prove the generalization to be true. Tell students that they must be able to read and pronounce any word they find and record for the activity. Adjust the amount and kind of reading material students will use and the number of words students should find, according to their needs. To expose each student to more words, ask students to share their lists aloud with a partner or the class. Keep the Prove It! lists to put in a class word bank or chart for future reference.

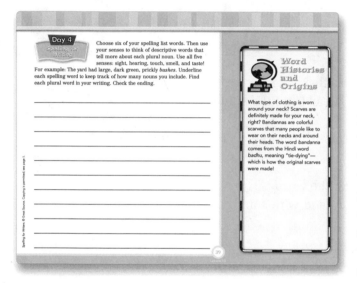

Have students choose six words from their spelling list. For each word, student will write a sentence that uses as many words as possible to describe the plural noun. Tell them to think about adjectives, or describing words that tell about size, shape, color, smell, and texture. Review the example on Student Book page 39, asking students which senses are represented.

Share these tips with students:

- Reread what you have written to see if it makes senses and complies with the directions for the activity.

- Look for any word omissions. (Sometimes the brain gets ahead of the hand!)

- Evaluate—can you squeeze in any more sensory words?

- Check for correct capitalization and end punctuation.

Proofreading Tip When proofreading, it is most effective to check one thing at a time. Tell students to make three passes through their sentences: one to check capitalization, one to check punctuation, and one to check spelling.

WORD HISTORY If needed, familiarize students with the process of tie-dyeing. (Clothes are dyed different colors by tying some of the material in knots to prevent the cloth inside the knot from absorbing the dye. The blank or white spots are what make tie-dye so unique.) Ask students what favorite colors they might choose to tie-dyeing T-shirts or other clothing. List students' responses and, when blue is mentioned, talk about different shades of blue (aqua, turquoise, baby blue, etc). Add *navy blue* to the discussion. Tell students that the British navy gave this color its name. *Navy blue* comes from the color of the British naval uniforms.

Day 5
Word Play and Posttest

Have students unscramble five of the pretest words. After students unscramble the words, have students figure out the riddle "You could have found me growing in different places all over the world 2,000 years ago. What am I?" by substituting the special letters with shapes around them into the coded message.

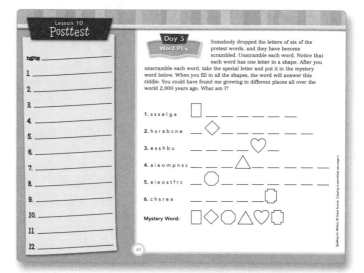

Answers

1. glasses
2. branches
3. bushes
4. companies
5. factories
6. arches

Mystery Word: grapes

Posttest Have students tear out the perforated posttest. Students should pair up with their buddies or partners and exchange School Lists (page 37 in Student Book). Students take turns testing each other on their respective spelling words. Collect the posttest sheets and record the correct response percentages. Mastery is 10 out of 12 words correct, or 80%. For students who do not achieve posttest mastery, see page xv in this Teacher's Edition. After the posttest, have students select one or two anchor words to help them remember the word feature in this lesson. Record the words on the "Anchor Words" poster and refer to them in the Review lesson.

Periodically, check writing samples from your students for transfer of the features that have been taught. The features for the last three lessons are as follows:

Lesson 8: R-Controlled Vowels
Lesson 9: Diphthongs
Lesson 10: Plurals (-*s*, -*es*, *y* to *i*)

Lesson 11

Past Tense. The past-tense verbs in this lesson represent three sounds but only two spellings (*kept, whined, supported*).

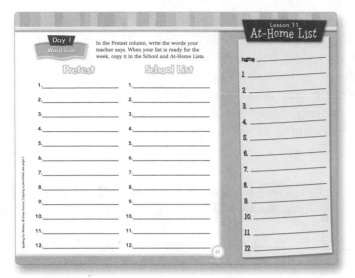

Day 1
Pretest and Word Lists

Before Photocopy the Answer Key/ Shopping List page (page 51 in this Teacher's Edition) for each student.

During Say each word in bold, read the context sentence, and repeat the word. Have students record the pretest words in the pretest column on page 41 of the Student Book.

After Distribute to students a copy of the Answer Key/Shopping List page so that they can correct their pretests.

- Students should cross out any misspelled words and write the correct spelling. Words that were correctly spelled can be replaced with words from the Shopping List. Identify the list from which students should choose their words. (See below.)

- Move around the room to be sure that each student has a list of twelve correctly spelled words, which they should copy into the School and At-Home Lists and the Sorting Boxes (page 51).

Pretest context sentences (spelling word in bold)

1. Dad **kept** his wallet in his back pocket.
2. Maggie **whined** because she did not want to wash the dishes.
3. The tea kettle **whistled** when the water boiled.
4. I was so tired last night that I **slept** for nine hours.
5. Kenny **tried** to jump over the hurdle.
6. Only the last two lines of the poem **rhymed**.
7. The bakery **supplied** the wedding cake.
8. The beams **supported** the weight of the building.
9. Jane **appeared** to be extremely upset yesterday.
10. The volcano **gushed** with lava when it erupted.
11. A car ran over the plastic bottle and **smashed** it.
12. In order to become a great pianist, John **practiced** every day.

At-Home List

Send the At-Home List home so that families can use the following activities with their students: word clues, word search, and past tense words.

NOTE The Shopping List provides words below grade level (the first two rows), at grade level (the middle two rows), and above grade level (the last two rows).

Name _____

1. kept	7. supplied
2. whined	8. supported
3. whistled	9. appeared
4. slept	10. gushed
5. tried	11. smashed
6. rhymed	12. practiced

Shopping List

patted	fixed	baked	clashed
pushed	hopped	spotted	danced
slammed	raised	kidded	followed
scared	depressed	iced	grabbed
applauded	accepted	cracked	accomplished
voiced	unbalanced	striped	deceased

Sorting Boxes

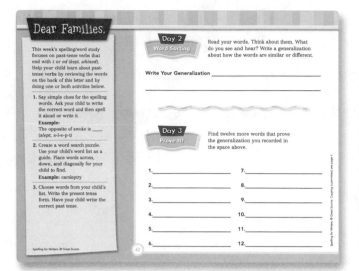

Have students look at the words carefully and decide for themselves a way or ways in which they can sort the words (do an open sort.) Once they have made their sorts, have them write a generalization about the words. How students think about the words shows you what they understand about them.

- If students have not reached consensus on their own, bring the class together to come to a consensus. Be certain to elicit ideas from the students that draw them to a common conclusion. You can use oversized word cards (CD-ROM) or a cut-up transparency (Transparency 11) and overhead to facilitate your model.

- Model how to sort the words into groups—verbs with the -ed past-tense ending and verbs with an irregular past-tense form. Remind students that these words (verbs) all show action that happened in the past.

- Next, focus on the words with -ed. Do another sort, this time grouping words according to the sound -ed represents— /d/, /t/, or /ĭd/.

- Have students place the two irregular pretest words, *kept* and *slept*, with those -ed words that have the /t/ sound at the end.

- Finally, have students identify spelling changes required for the addition of the -ed endings—dropping the extra *e*, doubling of final consonant, changing *y* to *i*.

- Have students write the generalization in their Student Book (page 42). You might also write the generalization on a sentence strip or poster to display for the duration of the lesson. Have students store their Sorting Boxes. (See page xi in this Teacher's Edition.)

Students should review the generalization: *Most verbs in the past tense are formed by adding -ed to the base word. Some verbs, however, have a completely different past-tense form. When words end in ed, the -ed can represent either /d/, /t/, or /ĭd/.* Then send them off to find in readable materials more examples that prove the generalization to be true. Tell students that they must be able to read and pronounce any word they find and record for the activity. Adjust the amount and kind of reading material students will use, according to their needs. To expose each student to more words, ask students to share their lists aloud with a partner or the class. Keep the Prove It! lists to put in a class word bank or chart for future reference.

Day 4
Spelling for Writing

Have students choose six words from their spelling list. They should write the spelling words as part of book titles and/or as part of the author names. Tell them to think about creative and funny book titles and author names in which they could use the spelling words. Review the example on Student Book page 43, asking students what the creative connection is. Another example is *They All Applauded* by Hans Together.

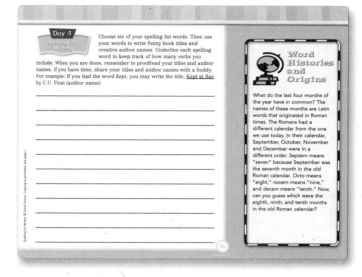

Share these tips with students:

- Reread what you have written to see if it makes senses and complies with the directions for the activity.

- Remember to underline the title of the book.

- Check for correct capitalization.

Proofreading Tip Tell students to check each word in their titles and author's names for correct capitalization. The first word and all important words in a title should be capitalized. Smaller, less important words are lowercase (e.g., articles and prepositions). The author's name should be capitalized.

WORD HISTORY Tell students that like the months September, October, November, and December; the month of July also has an interesting and important origin. *July* is an important month because it is named for the person who made the calendar we use today. At one time, the month of *July* was called "Quintilis" because it was the fifth month in the old Gregorian calendar. Explain to students that *quintus* means "fifth." When Julius Caesar was born in July 44 BCE, the month was renamed to honor him. Caesar was such a powerful and influential statesman that he reorganized the calendar to give us 12 months, 365 days. And, he made every fourth year a leap year! Caesar made each month have 30 or 31 days, except for February. This is called the Julian calendar. Ask students to infer why it's called the Julian calendar.

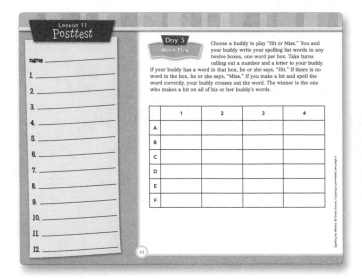

Have students find a partner to play "Hit or Miss." Each student should write their spelling list words in any 12 of the 24 boxes of the grid, one word per box. Suggest that they insert their words randomly. Have partners alternate calling out a number (from one to four) and a letter (from A to F) to identify a box in their partner's grid. If a partner has a word in that box, he or she says, "Hit." If there is no word in the box, he or she says, "Miss." If one of the partners makes a hit and spells the word correctly, the other partner crosses out the word. The winner is the partner who makes a hit on all of the other partner's words.

Posttest Have students tear out the perforated posttest. Students should pair up with their buddies or partners and exchange School Lists (page 41 in Student Book). Students take turns testing each other on their respective spelling words. Collect the posttest sheets and record the correct response percentages. Mastery is 10 out of 12 words correct, or 80%. For students who do not achieve posttest mastery, see page xv in this Teacher's Edition.

After the posttest, have students select one or two anchor words to help them remember the word feature in this lesson. Record the words on the "Anchor Words" poster and refer to them in the Review lesson.

Lesson 12 — Compound Words.

A compound word is made by putting two words together: *background, whenever,* and *storybook.*

Day 1
Pretest and Word Lists

Day 1
Word Lists

In the Pretest column, write the words your teacher says. When your list is ready for the week, copy it in the School and At-Home Lists.

Pretest

1.
2.
3.
4.
5.
6.
7.
8.
9.
10.
11.
12.

School List

1.
2.
3.
4.
5.
6.
7.
8.
9.
10.
11.
12.

Lesson 12
At-Home List

name

1.
2.
3.
4.
5.
6.
7.
8.
9.
10.
11.
12.

45

Before Photocopy the Answer Key/ Shopping List page (page 56 in this Teacher's Edition) for each student.

During Say each word in bold, read the context sentence, and repeat the word. Have students record the pretest words in the pretest column on page 45 of the Student Book.

After Distribute to students a copy of the Answer Key/Shopping List page so that they can correct their pretests.

- Students should cross out any misspelled words and write the correct spelling. Words that were correctly spelled can be replaced with words from the Shopping List. Identify the list from which students should choose their words. (See below.)

- Move around the room to be sure that each student has a list of twelve correctly spelled words, which they should copy into the School and At-Home Lists and the Sorting Boxes (page 56).

Pretest context sentences (spelling word in bold)

1. I **always** brush my teeth before going to bed.
2. The **background** of the photograph was too dark.
3. In the summer, bees are **everywhere**!
4. **Whenever** I need some energy, I just eat some fruit.
5. Jim and Jason always eat lunch **together**.
6. The train moves up and down the **railroad** tracks.
7. The teacher will read the class a **storybook**.
8. **Everyone** was excited to see the movie star.
9. There are swings and slides in the **playground**.
10. Since the elevator was broken, we had to walk **downstairs**.
11. Many houses collapsed during the **earthquake**.
12. I could not **understand** the math problem.

At-Home List Send the At-Home List home so that families can use the following activities with their students: match up word parts, make words, fill in word parts.

NOTE The Shopping List provides words below grade level (the first two rows), at grade level (the middle two rows), and above grade level (the last two rows).

Name ______________________________

Answer Key

1. always
2. background
3. everywhere
4. whenever
5. together
6. railroad
7. storybook
8. everyone
9. playground
10. downstairs
11. earthquake
12. understand

Shopping List

anything	airplane	campfire	grandmother
baseball	someday	somehow	birthday
homesick	everybody	overcome	newscast
forever	underwater	shoreline	shinbone
masterpiece	broadcast	touchdown	flashlight
cheerleader	grapefruit	wheelchair	firecracker

Sorting Boxes

Day 2
Word Sorting

Model for students how to look at all the words (you may use all the words for the pretest and the Shopping List words). They should discover with you that all the words are compound words, or words that are formed by two words coming together to make a new word that has its own meaning. You can use oversized word cards (CD-ROM) or a cut-up transparency (Transparency 12) and overhead to facilitate your model.

- Have students do an open sort of the words, finding their own ways of grouping them. If students need suggestions to start their thinking, offer the following: words related to the outdoors, words related to people.

- Have students write the generalization in their Student Book (page 46). You might also write the generalization on a sentence strip or poster to display for the duration of the lesson. Leave room for students to add some of their Prove It! words from Day 3.

- Have students store their Sorting Boxes. (See page xi in this Teacher's Edition.)

Day 3
Prove It!

Students should review the generalization: *Compound words are formed by two words coming together to make a new word that has its own meaning.* Then send them off to find in readable materials more examples that prove the generalization to be true. Tell students that they must be able to read and pronounce any word they find and record for the activity. Adjust the amount and kind of reading material students will use, according to their needs. Keep the Prove It! lists to put in a class word bank or chart for future reference.

NOTE The words in this lesson are closed compound words, compounds spelled as one word. Students might identify open or hyphenated compound words, such as *search engine*, *bald eagle*, or *baby-sit*. Put those words in their own categories. Students may discover some variation from one dictionary to another, regarding whether a word is a closed, open, or hyphenated compound.

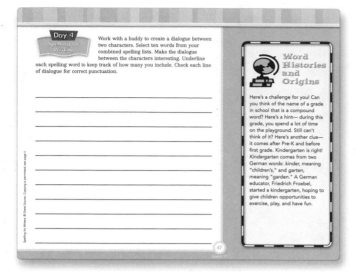

Day 4
Spelling for Writing

Have student pairs choose ten words from their combined spelling lists and create a dialogue between two characters. Tell students that their dialogue could be about anything—it may be funny, scary, serious, or sad. Students should underline their spelling words to help them keep track of how many they are able to include.

Remind students of the elements of a dialogue:

- The words should sound just like the character's voice.

- Any dialogue should be enclosed in quotation marks.

- Punctuation (comma, period, exclamation point, question mark) for the speaker's dialogue goes inside the closing quotation mark.

- End punctuation should help convey the feelings of the speaker.

- The speaker tag (which tells who spoke and how) should also help convey the feelings of the speaker (*cried, pleaded, laughed, whispered*).

Proofreading Tip Have students check their dialogue for correct punctuation. If students work in pairs, one student can read the speaker's words while the other student looks to see that those words—and only those words—are enclosed in quotation marks.

WORD HISTORY Ask students if they can think of any names of games that are compound words. As students respond, list their words. (Common responses may include *football, basketball, baseball*.) Add *hopscotch* if it is not suggested. If students are not familiar with hopscotch, you may briefly describe the game—a children's game in which the players hop over lines of a figure drawn on the ground and pick up an object that is thrown or kicked into one of the numbered squares of the figure. Have students divide the word *hopscotch* word into its two word parts—*hop* and *scotch*. Explain to students that *scotch* means "scratch." When you play hopscotch, you hop over the lines you scratched on the ground.

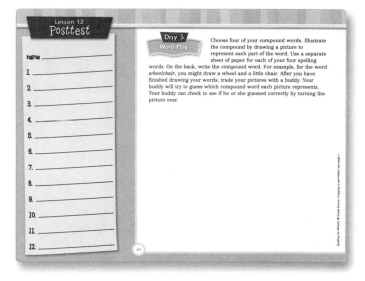

Day 5
Word Play and Posttest

Have students illustrate four of their compound words by drawing a picture to represent each part of the word. Students should use a separate sheet of paper for each of their compound words. Remind students to write the compound word on the back of each picture. After students finish drawing pictures for their compound words, have each student trade pictures with a partner. Each partner tries to guess which compound word each picture represents. Students can check to see if their guesses are correct by turning the pictures over. Save the pictures to use as an independent activity in a word center.

Posttest Have students tear out the perforated posttest. Students should pair up with their buddies or partners and exchange School Lists (page 45 in the Student Book). Students take turns testing each other on their respective spelling words. Collect the posttest sheets and record the correct response percentages. Mastery is 10 out of 12 words correct, or 80%. For students who do not achieve posttest mastery, see page xv in this Teacher's Edition.

After the posttest, have students select one or two anchor words to help them remember the word feature in this lesson. Record the words on the "Anchor Words" poster and refer to them in the Review lesson.

Lesson 13 — Doubled Consonants (before endings).
When the base word has one short vowel sound and ends in a consonant, the consonant is doubled before adding the ending or suffix.

Before Photocopy the Answer Key/Shopping List page (page 61 in this Teacher's Edition) for each student.

During Say each word in bold, read the context sentence, and repeat the word. Have students record the pretest words in the pretest column on page 49 of the Student Book.

After Distribute to students a copy of the Answer Key/Shopping List page so that they can correct their pretests.

- Students should cross out any misspelled words and write the correct spelling. Words that were correctly spelled can be replaced with words from the Shopping List. Identify the list from which students should choose their words. (See below.)

- Be sure that each student has a list of twelve correctly spelled words, which they should copy into the School and At-Home Lists and the Sorting Boxes (page 61).

Pretest context sentences (spelling word in bold)

1. I *skipped* over the puddle of water.
2. The cost of *shipping* the package was $5.95.
3. Dad *grinned* when I made a funny comment.
4. The *shopper* had so many bags that she could barely carry them!
5. The audience *clapped* at the end of the play.
6. The *drummer* marches at the back of the marching band.
7. My older brother was *bragging* about his new car.
8. My little sister *dragged* the heavy bags into the house.
9. My jacket *zipper* is stuck!
10. The *fitter* had a lot of work to do backstage at the fashion show.
11. The employees are *tagging* the new merchandise.
12. The teacher got the class's attention by *snapping* his fingers.

At-Home List Send the At-Home List home so that families can use the following activities with their students: match up word parts and categories.

NOTE The Shopping List provides words below grade level (the first two rows), at grade level (the middle two rows), and above grade level (the last two rows).

Name _____

Answer Key

1. skipped	7. bragging
2. shipping	8. dragged
3. grinned	9. zipper
4. shopper	10. fitter
5. clapped	11. tagging
6. drummer	12. snapping

Shopping List

stepping	planner	bragged	jogger
jammed	humming	dipper	hugging
swimming	skidded	stopper	petted
beginning	chatter	trimmed	spotted
transmitter	trapping	skipper	shredding
submitted	wrapper	nabbed	throbbing

Sorting Boxes

Lesson 13

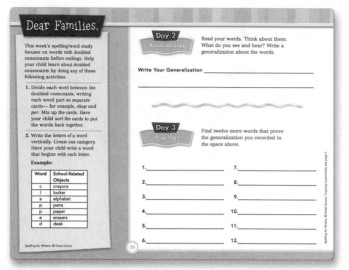

Day 2
Word Sorting

Have students look at the words carefully and decide for themselves a way or ways in which they can sort the words (do an open sort.) Once they have made their sorts, have them write a generalization about the words. How students think about the words shows you what they understand about them. The written generalization is evidence of their thought process.

- If students have not reached consensus, bring the class together to come to a consensus. Be certain to elicit ideas from the students that draw them to a common conclusion. You can use oversized word cards (CD-ROM) or a cut up transparency (Transparency 13) and overhead to facilitate your model.

- Model for students a way to sort, using all the words. The three general categories for the sorting should be *-ed*, *-ing*, and *-er* endings/suffixes.

- After students successfully make their sorts, guide them to notice features of words that have double consonants before the ending or suffix. Help students identify the base word for each word. Then note the short vowel sound each word has.

- Model for students how to make a statement about how all their words were sorted: *When the base word has one short vowel sound and ends in a consonant, the consonant is doubled before adding the ending or suffix.*

- Have students write the generalization in their Student Book (page 50). You might also write the generalization on a sentence strip or poster to display for the duration of the lesson. Leave room for students to add some of their Prove It! words from Day 3.

- Have students store their Sorting Boxes. (See page xi in this Teacher's Edition.)

Day 3
Prove It!

Students should review the generalization: *When the base word has one short vowel sound and ends in a consonant, the consonant is doubled before adding the ending or suffix.* Then send them off to find in readable materials more examples that prove the generalization to be true. Tell students that they must be able to read and pronounce any word they find and record for the activity. Adjust the amount and kind of reading material students will use and the number of words students should use, according to their needs. To expose each student to more words, ask students to share their lists aloud with a partner or the class. Keep the Prove It! lists to put in a class word bank or chart for future reference.

Day 4
Spelling for Writing

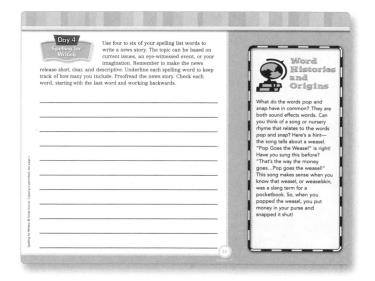

Have students choose four to six words from their spelling lists to create a news story. Tell students that the news story can be based on current issues in the news, about an eye-witnessed event, or from students' imagination. Students should underline their spelling words to help them keep track of how many they are able to include.

Remind students of the elements of a news story:

- It should have an attention-getting headline.

- It always contains the answers to the *5Ws—who, what, where, when,* and *why.*

- It should include some direct quotations regarding the topic.

- The wording should be concise, but enticing to the reader.

Proofreading Tip Suggest that students proofread their news story by checking each word from the end to the beginning. When they encounter a word that has an ending, they should check to see whether the consonant should be doubled.

WORD HISTORY Students may enjoy having another explanation of the song "Pop Goes the Weasel." Tell students that this old English singing game has nothing to do with the animal called *weasel.* The "weasel" that goes "pop" may have been a tool used by English hatters, tailors, and cobblers. When money was in short supply, they "popped," or pawned, their weasels.

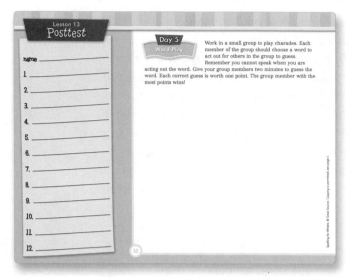

Have student teams play charades. Put all the word cards for this week in a hat. Group the students into several small teams. A student from each team picks a word card from the hat and tries to act out (without speaking) what the word represents to his or her teammates. The team has two minutes to guess the correct word. Each correct guess is worth one point. The team with the most points after all the words have been acted out wins the game.

Posttest Have students tear out the perforated posttest. Students should pair up with their buddies or partners and exchange School Lists (page 49 in the Student Book). Students take turns testing each other on their respective spelling words. Collect the posttest sheets and record the correct response percentages. Mastery is 10 out of 12 words correct, or 80%. For students who do not achieve posttest mastery, see page xv in this Teacher's Edition.

After the posttest, have students select one or two anchor words to help them remember the word feature in this lesson. Record the words on the "Anchor Words" poster and refer to them in the Review lesson.

Periodically, check writing samples from your students for transfer of the features that have been taught. The features for the last three lessons are as follows:

Lesson 11: Past Tense
Lesson 12: Compound Words
Lesson 13: Doubled Consonants (before endings)

Lesson 14 Prefixes and Suffixes.
When a prefix or suffix is added to a word, the meaning of the word changes (*unable*, *playful*).

Day 1
Pretest and Word Lists

Before Photocopy the Answer Key/ Shopping List page (page 66 in this Teacher's Edition) for each student.

During Say each word in bold, read the context sentence, and repeat the word. Have students record the pretest words in the pretest column on page 53 of the Student Book.

After Distribute to students a copy of the Answer Key/Shopping List page so that they can correct their pretests.

- Students should cross out any misspelled words and write the correct spelling. Words that were correctly spelled can be replaced with words from the Shopping List. Identify the list from which students should choose their words. (See below.)

- Be sure that each student has a list of twelve correctly spelled words, which they should copy into the School and At-Home Lists and the Sorting Boxes (page 66).

Pretest context sentences (spelling word in bold)

1. The kitten was very **playful**.
2. I felt nervous and **uneasy** during the thunderstorm.
3. I cannot **recall** where I left my math book.
4. They were so noisy that I had to **retell** my story three times!
5. My little sister goes to **preschool** every day.
6. We take a **pretest** to practice for the chapter test.
7. Mom is **unable** to sing, although she tries all the time.
8. If you **unplug** the TV, it won't work.
9. I am **hopeful** that I passed the test.
10. Having a ruler in math class is very **useful**.
11. My piano lessons were **prepaid**, so I didn't have to pay each week.
12. The detective will **uncover** the truth about the mystery.

At-Home List Send the At-Home List home so that families can use the following activities with their students: word tally, word crosses.

NOTE The Shopping List provides words below grade level (the first two rows), at grade level (the middle two rows), and above grade level (the last two rows) that still use the feature (prefixes and suffixes).

Name _____

Answer Key

1. playful	7. unable
2. uneasy	8. unplug
3. recall	9. hopeful
4. retell	10. useful
5. preschool	11. prepaid
6. pretest	12. uncover

Shopping List

untie	careful	unsafe	reread
redo	refill	loveable	retry
recopy	joyful	enjoyable	skillful
graceful	helpful	spreadable	unhook
colorful	regroup	wonderful	unthinkable
careless	unusual	agreeable	revision

Sorting Boxes

Day 2
Word Sorting

Have students look at the words carefully and decide for themselves a way or ways in which they can sort the words (do an open sort). Once they have made their sorts, have them write a generalization about the words. How students think about the words shows you what they understand about them. The written generalization is evidence of their thought process.

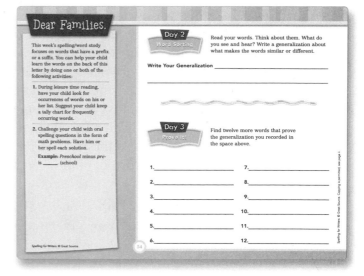

- After students do an open sort, bring the class together to come to consensus. If students have not or cannot come to consensus, model for them a way to sort using all the words. You can use oversized word cards (CD-ROM) or a cut-up transparency (Transparency 14) and overhead to facilitate your model.

- The two general categories for the sorting should be words with prefixes and words with suffixes. After students successfully make their sorts, guide them to notice the different prefixes and suffixes.

- Help students identify each base word. Discuss the meaning of the base word compared to the affixed word's meaning.

un- means "not"	*–ful* means "full of"
re- means "again" or "back"	*–able* means "able to"
pre- means "before"	*–less* means "less"

- Model for students how to make a statement about how all their words were sorted: *When a prefix or suffix is added to a word, the meaning of the word changes.*

- Have students write the generalization in their Student Book (page 54). You might also write the generalization on a sentence strip or poster to display for the duration of the lesson. Leave room for students to add some of their Prove It! words from Day 3.

- Have students store their Sorting Boxes. (See page xi in this Teacher's Edition.)

Students should review the generalization from Day 2: *When a prefix or suffix is added to a word, the meaning of the word changes.* Then send them off to find in readable materials more examples that prove the generalization to be true.

Day 3
Prove It!

Tell students that they must be able to read and pronounce any word they find and record for the activity. Adjust the amount and kind of reading material students will use and the number of words they should find, according to their needs. Keep the Prove It! lists to put in a class word bank or chart for future reference.

> NOTE Students may find some words that begin or end like the affixed spelling words but that do not have a prefix or a suffix: for example, *unit* or *table*. Help students examine the words by asking them to break apart the words. They should notice that when *un-* or *-able* is removed, the part that is left is not a meaningful word part.

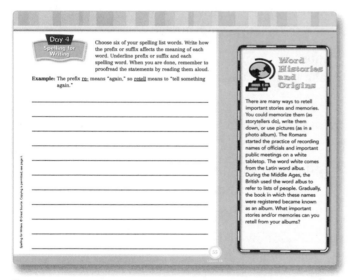

Day 4
Spelling for Writing

Have students choose six words from their spelling lists and write a statement for each word explaining how the prefix or suffix changes the meaning of the base word. Encourage students to use a dictionary if needed. Students should underline their spelling words.

Example: The prefix *un-* means "not," so *unable* means "not able."

Proofreading Tip Suggest that students use the proofreading strategy of reading aloud. This will help slow students' reading rate so that they can check each word individually. Students can whisper so as not to disturb their neighbors.

WORD HISTORY Students will no doubt share many stories that they can recall from their albums. Share the history of the word *story*. The word *story* is from Anglo-Norman *estorie* and Latin *historia*, both meaning "account of events, narrative, history." Point out that originally, *story* was associated with a factual account of past events, but since the seventeenth century, the use of *story* has been associated more closely with fictional narratives. Encourage students to name their favorite story (fictional narrative).

Day 5
Word Play and Posttest

Have student unscramble the twelve pretest words. Remind students to read each clue carefully so they can unscramble the words more easily.

Answers:

1. preschool	7. unplug
2. hopeful	8. retell
3. recall	9. uneasy
4. useful	10. uncover
5. playful	11. unable
6. pretest	12. prepaid

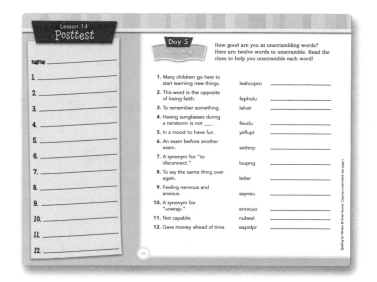

Posttest Have students tear out the perforated posttest. Students should pair up with their buddies or partners and exchange School Lists (page 53 in the Student Book). Students take turns testing each other on their respective spelling words. Collect the posttest sheets and record the correct response percentages. Mastery is 10 out of 12 words correct, or 80%. For students who do not achieve posttest mastery, see page xv in this Teacher's Edition.

After the posttest, have students select one or two anchor words to help them remember the word feature in this lesson. Record the words on the "Anchor Words" poster and refer to them in the Review lesson.

Lesson 15 Derivations and Relations Words that are related may sound different but are similar in spelling (reduce/reduction).

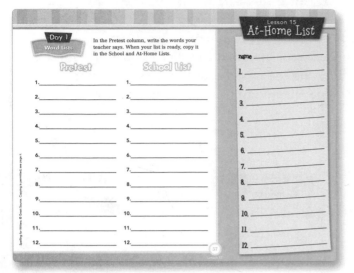

Before Photocopy the Answer Key/ Shopping List page (page 71 in this Teacher's Edition) for each student.

During Say each word in bold, read the context sentence, and repeat the word. Have students record the pretest words in the pretest column on page 57 of the Student Book.

After Distribute to students a copy of the Answer Key/Shopping List page so that they can correct their pretests.

- Students should cross out any misspelled words and write the correct spelling. If one word in a pair is misspelled, consider the pair wrong. Word pairs that were correctly spelled can be replaced with word pairs from the Shopping List.

- Be sure that each student has a list of twelve correctly spelled words, which they should copy into the School and At-Home Lists and the Sorting Boxes (page 71).

Pretest context sentences (spelling word in bold)

1. I play my guitar to **reduce** stress.
2. The **reduction** of stress can be achieved in many ways.
3. The network will **televise** the concert.
4. The concert will be shown on **television**.
5. **Nature** is full of beautiful flowers and exotic animals.
6. Animals and flowers are **natural** elements on Earth.
7. A match will cause gasoline to **ignite**.
8. Gasoline and matches produce a fast **ignition**.
9. The musician will **compose** a song.
10. The musician's **composition** won an award.
11. Our mayor will **declare** new city laws.
12. Our mayor has an important **declaration** to make.

At-Home List Send the At-Home List home so that families can use the following activities with their students: related words sentence, word crosses.

NOTE The Shopping List provides words below grade level (the first two rows), at grade level (the middle two rows), and above grade level (the last two rows) that still use the feature (derivations and relations).

Name _____

Answer Key

1. reduce	7. ignite
2. reduction	8. ignition
3. televise	9. compose
4. television	10. composition
5. nature	11. declare
6. natural	12. declaration

Shopping List

install	hospital	metal	produce
installation	hospitality	metallic	production
invite	angel	predict	extreme
invitation	angelic	prediction	extremity
number	athlete	mischief	know
numerous	athletic	mischievous	knowledge

Sorting Boxes

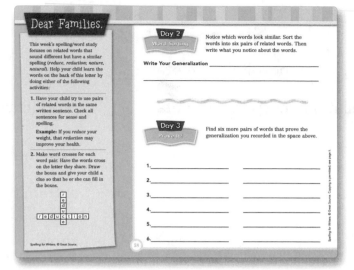

Day 2
Word Sorting

Have students look at the words carefully and decide for themselves a way or ways in which they can sort the words (do an open sort). Once they have made their sorts, have them write a generalization about the words. How students think about the words shows you what they understand about them. The written generalization is evidence of their thought process.

- After students do an open sort, bring the class together to come to consensus. If students have not or cannot come to consensus, model for them a way to sort using all the words. You can use oversized word cards (CD-ROM) or a cut-up transparency (Transparency 15) and overhead to facilitate your model.

- The general category for the sorting is related word pairs. After students successfully pair the words, help students pronounce each word in a pair. Ask them to explain what they notice. (There is a vowel-sound change.) Then guide students to notice the similar spelling the word pairs have. There is a sound change but *not* a spelling change.

- Model for students how to make a statement about how all their words were sorted: *Words that are related may sound different but are similar in spelling.*

- Emphasize the spelling-meaning connection between words as a strategy for spelling. For example, one knows to use an *a* in *hospital* because of the short *a* sound in *hospitality*. Ask students to explain how this works in other words.

- Have students write the generalization in their Student Book (page 58). You might also write the generalization on a sentence strip or poster to display for the duration of the lesson. Leave room for students to add some of their Prove It! words from Day 3.

- Have students store their Sorting Boxes. (See page xi in this Teacher's Edition.)

Day 3
Prove It!

Students should review the generalization from Day 2: *Words that are related may sound different but are similar in spelling.* Then send them off to find in readable materials more examples that prove the generalization to be true. (Have them try for six pairs of words). Tell students that they must be able to read and pronounce any word they find and record for the activity. Adjust the amount and kind of reading material students will use and the number of words they should find, according to their needs. To expose each student to more words, ask students to share their lists aloud with a partner or the class. Keep the Prove It! lists to put in a class word bank or chart for future reference.

NOTE Suggest that students start with their math or social studies textbooks to find content-area word pairs such as *divide/division*, *add/addition*, and *history/historic*.

Day 4
Spelling for Writing

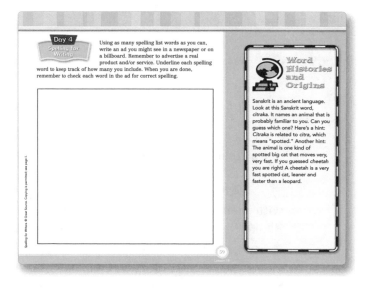

Have students use as many spelling list words as they can to write a brief news paper or billboard ad. Tell students that the product/service they will advertise must be either something they have seen, heard about, or read about in books or magazines. Students should underline their spelling words to help them keep track of how many they include.

Remind students of the elements of an effective advertisement:

- The purpose of an advertisement is to persuade.

- Use emotionally charged language and words with positive connotations to encourage customers to buy your product.

- The tone should be energetic.

- Punctuation should convey the writer's emotions.

Proofreading Tip Explain to students that accurate copy is a courtesy to the reader. Mistakes can distract a reader and take attention away from the writer's message. Students should check the spelling of each word in their advertisements. To help focus students' attention on individual words, suggest that they touch a pencil point to each word.

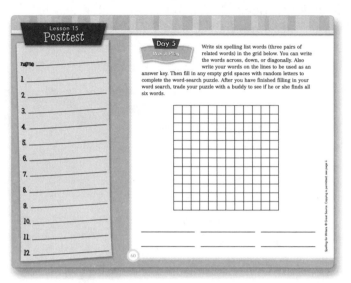

Word Play and Posttest

Students will create a word-search puzzle that includes six spelling list words (three pairs of related words) for a partner to solve.

- Tell students to write their words in the grid on Student Book page 60 and on the lines below the grid (to provide an answer key).

- In the puzzle, students can write their words across, down, or diagonally. Tell them to fill in any empty grid spaces with random letters.

- When the word-search puzzles are ready, have students find a partner and trade puzzles. Each partner finds and circles the hidden words.

Posttest Have students tear out the perforated posttest. Students should pair up with their buddies or partners and exchange School Lists (page 57 in the Student Book). Students take turns testing each other on their respective spelling words. Collect the posttest sheets and record the correct response percentages. Mastery is 10 out of 12 words correct, or 80%. For students who do not achieve posttest mastery, see page xv in this Teacher's Edition.

After the posttest, have students select one or two anchor words to help them remember the word feature in this lesson. Record the words on the "Anchor Words" poster and refer to them in the Review lesson.

Lesson 16 · Consonant Blends.

When a consonant comes before *l* or *r*, the sounds are blended together (*blade*, *grapes*).

Day 1
Pretest and Word Lists

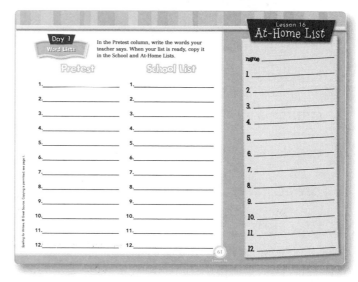

Before Photocopy the Answer Key/ Shopping List page (page 76 in this Teacher's Edition) for each student.

During Say each word in bold, read the context sentence, and repeat the word. Have students record the pretest words in the pretest column on page 61 of the Student Book.

After Distribute to students a copy of the Answer Key/Shopping List page so that they can correct their pretests.

- Students should cross out any misspelled words and write the correct spelling. Words that were correctly spelled can be replaced with words from the Shopping List. Identify the list from which students should choose their words. (See below.)

- Be sure that each student has a list of twelve correctly spelled words, which they should copy into the School and At-Home Lists and the Sorting Boxes (page 76).

Pretest context sentences (spelling word in bold)

1. The **blade** of the knife is sharp.
2. Purple **grapes** hung from the vine in clusters.
3. Let me **glance** at this page for a moment.
4. He went to look for frogs in the **creek**.
5. **Greed** is the love of money.
6. The couple wrapped their baby in a soft **blanket**.
7. I like **crisp**, not soft, cookies.
8. The **glare** from the car's headlights scared the deer.
9. The stars were **glowing** in the night sky.
10. The new bridge will enable cars to **cross** over the river.
11. Dad knew I lied about doing my homework, and he called my **bluff**.
12. There was a **crowd** outside the movie theater.

At-Home List Send the At-Home List home so that families can use the following activities with their students: word completions, word boxes, word hunt.

NOTE The Shopping List provides words below grade level (the first two rows), at grade level (the middle two rows), and above grade level (the last two rows) that still use the feature (consonant blends).

Name _____

Answer Key

1. blade	7. crisp
2. grapes	8. glare
3. glance	9. glowing
4. creek	10. cross
5. greed	11. bluff
6. blanket	12. crowd

Shopping List

crack	crops	glove	glitter
blow	glass	crook	crew
blind	globe	block	crayon
gloomy	glue	crowded	blood
blockade	blossom	glossary	cricket
crystal	glaze	glimpse	Greece

Sorting Boxes

Day 2
Word Sorting

Have students look at the words carefully and decide for themselves a way or ways in which they can sort the words (do an open sort). Once they have made their sorts, have them write a generalization about the words. How students think about the words shows you what they understand about them. The written generalization is evidence of their thought process.

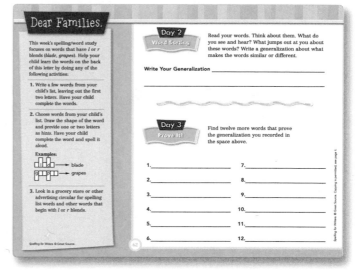

- After students do an open sort, bring the class together. If students have not or cannot come to consensus, model for them a way to sort using all the words. You can use oversized word cards (CD-ROM) or a cut-up transparency (Transparency 16) and overhead to facilitate your model.

- The two general categories for the sorting should be words beginning with *l* blends and *r* blends. After students successfully make their sorts, guide them to notice the blended sound that the side-by-side consonants represent. Note that both consonants can be heard, but they are smoothed together.

- Model for students how to make a statement about how all their words were sorted: *Two side-by-side consonants blend their sounds together, although you can hear both sounds.*

- Have students write the generalization in their Student Book (page 62). You might also write the generalization on a sentence strip or poster to display for the duration of the lesson. Leave room for students to add some of their Prove It! words from Day 3.

- Have students store their Sorting Boxes. (See page xi in this Teacher's Edition.)

Day 3
Prove It!

Students should review the generalization from Day 2: *Two side-by-side consonants can blend their sounds together, although you can hear both sounds.* Then send them off to find in readable materials more examples that prove the generalization to be true. Tell students that they must be able to read and pronounce any word they find and record for the activity. Adjust the amount and kind of reading material students will use and the number of words they should find, according to their needs. To expose each student to more words, ask students to share their lists aloud with a partner or the class. Keep the Prove It! lists to put in a class word bank or chart for future reference.

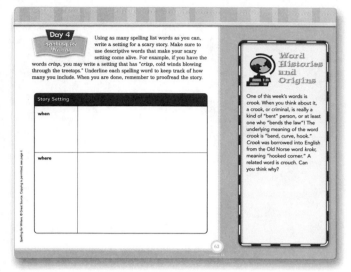

Day 4
Spelling for Writing

Using as many spelling list words as you can, write a setting for a scary story. Make sure to use descriptive words that make your scary setting come alive. For example, if you have the words *crisp*, you may write a setting that has "*crisp*, cold winds blowing through the treetops." Underline each spelling word to keep track of how many you include. When you are done, remember to proofread the story.

Story Setting

when	
where	

Word Histories and Origins

One of this week's words is *crook*. When you think about it, a crook, or criminal, is really a kind of "bent" person, or at least one who "bends the law"! The underlying meaning of the word crook is "bend, curve, hook." *Crook* was borrowed into English from the Old Norse word *krokr*, meaning "hooked corner." A related word is *crouch*. Can you think why?

63

Have students use as many spelling list words as possible to describe the setting for a scary story. They don't have to write the story, just tell about what the place looks like and the sounds characters might hear. Point out that precise adjectives will help them create their scary setting. Students should underline their spelling words to help them keep track of how many they include.

Give students these tips for writing a description of a setting:

- Use words that appeal to the five senses.

- Include time as an element of the setting—years ago, the dead of winter, and so on.

- Draw a picture first, if it helps inspire some writing.

Proofreading Tip Remind students that reading and proofreading are different. Ask students to suggest ways that they can slow their reading pace to examine every word (read aloud, touch a pencil point to each letter).

WORD HISTORY Share another word of Norse origin with students— *window*. The word *window* originated with the Norse word *vindauga*, meaning "wind-eye." When the Norse built their homes, they created an opening at the top for smoke to escape. Over time, the location of the window moved down to the wall so people could see out of it. Why is "wind-eye" an apt name?

Have students play a game of "What's My Word?" with a partner. Each partner chooses three or four of his or her spelling list words. Partners take turns trying to guess the other partner's words by asking their partner yes or no questions. Examples of appropriate questions follow:

- Is the word a noun?

- Does your word have more than five letters?

- Does the word have one syllable?

You can also play "What's My Word?" with the whole class, if you choose to do so. Gather the word cards from Day 2's sorting activities. Select one card at a time. Students ask you yes or no questions in order to guess the word. If students don't guess the word in a reasonable amount of time (say, within ten questions), offer clues to them.

Posttest Have students tear out the perforated posttest. Students should pair up with their buddies or partners and exchange School Lists (page 61 in the Student Book). Students take turns testing each other on their respective spelling words. Collect the posttest sheets and record the correct response percentages. Mastery is 10 out of 12 words correct, or 80%. For students who do not achieve posttest mastery, see page xv in this Teacher's Edition.

After the posttest, have students select one or two anchor words to help them remember the word feature in this lesson. Record the words on the "Anchor Words" poster and refer to them in the Review lesson.

Periodically, check writing samples from your students for transfer of the word features that have been taught. The features for the last three lessons follow:

Lesson 14: Prefixes and Suffixes
Lesson 15: Derivations and Relations
Lesson 16: Consonant Blends

Day 1

Pretest and Word Lists

Before Photocopy the Answer Key/ Shopping List page (page 81 in this Teacher's Edition) for each student.

During Say each word in bold, read the context sentence, and repeat the word. Have students record the pretest words in the pretest column on page 65 of the Student Book.

After Distribute to students a copy of the Answer Key/Shopping List page so that they can correct their pretests.

- Students should cross out any misspelled words and write the correct spelling. Words that were correctly spelled can be replaced with words from the Shopping List. Identify the list from which students should choose their words. (See below.)

- Be sure that each student has a list of twelve correctly spelled words, which they should copy into the School and At-Home Lists and the Sorting Boxes (page 81).

Pretest context sentences (spelling word in bold)

1. The sick puppy is **thinner** than the healthy dog.
2. My dad tells **funnier** jokes than my mom does.
3. That Chihuahua is the **littlest** dog I have ever seen!
4. Hot glue is **stickier** than paste.
5. My sister's hair is **curlier** than mine.
6. My **happiest** moment was when I scored the winning goal!
7. A needle is **sharper** than a toothpick.
8. The **busiest** time to shop is around the winter holidays.
9. Are elephants the **heaviest** animals on Earth?
10. An elephant is **heavier** than a mouse.
11. A siren is much **louder** than a bird's chirp.
12. I am **braver** than my little sister.

At-Home List Send the At-Home List home so that families can use the following activities with their students: comparative/superlative words, riddles.

NOTE The Shopping List provides words below grade level (the first two rows), at grade level (the middle two rows), and above grade level (the last two rows) that still use the feature (comparatives and superlatives).

Name _____

Answer Key

1. thinner
2. funnier
3. littlest
4. stickier
5. curlier
6. happiest
7. sharper
8. busiest
9. heaviest
10. heavier
11. louder
12. braver

Shopping List

madder	sillier	luckiest	biggest
easier	flatter	finest	tallest
thinnest	nastier	funniest	dirtier
fancier	gentler	flakier	dirtiest
unluckiest	shakiest	fresher	clumsiest
steadier	abler	noisiest	widest

Sorting Boxes

Day 2
Word Sorting

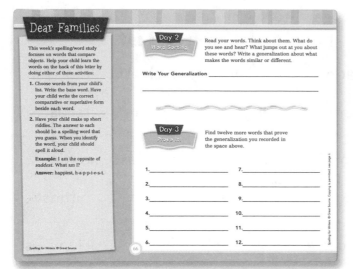

Have students look at the words carefully and decide for themselves a way or ways in which they can sort the words (do an open sort). Once they have made their sorts, have them write a generalization about the words. How students think about the words shows you what they understand about them.

- After students do an open sort, bring the class together to come to consensus about what the words have in common. If students have not or cannot come to consensus, model a way to sort all the words. You can use oversized word cards (CD-ROM) or a cut-up transparency (Transparency 17) and overhead for the demonstration.

- The two general categories for the sorting should be words ending with *-er* and *-est*. After students successfully make their sorts, guide them to notice that all the words are describing words, or adjectives.

- Help students decide which group of words can be used to compare two things and which group can be used to compare more than two things.

- Work with students to identify the base word for each spelling list word. Ask students to describe any changes that are required before an ending is added (final consonant doubled; *y* to *i* change; drop *e*).

- If it will help your students, discuss why and when spelling changes are necessary. (They preserve the vowel sound when a word is divided between two consonants, as in *thin-ner*. They prevent double letters that look strange, such as "stickyyer.")

- Model for students how to make a statement about how all their words were sorted: *Adjectives that compare two things have an -er ending, and adjectives that describe three or more things have an -est ending.*

- If appropriate for your class, introduce the terms *comparative* (a word that compares two things, such as *cleaner*) and *superlative* (a word that compares three or more things, such as *cleanest*). The base word, *clean*, is called the *declarative*.

- Have students write the generalization in their Student Book (page 66). You might also write the generalization on a sentence strip or poster to display for the duration of the lesson. Leave room for students to add some of their Prove It! words from Day 3.

- Have students store their Sorting Boxes. (See page xi in this Teacher's Edition.)

82 Lesson 17

Day 3

Prove It!

Students should review the generalization from Day 2: *Adjectives that compare two things have an -er ending, and adjectives that describe three or more things have an -est ending.* Then send them off to find in readable materials more examples that prove the generalization to be true. Tell students that they must be able to read and pronounce any word they find and record for the activity. Adjust the amount and kind of reading material students will use and the number of words they should find, according to their needs. To expose each student to more words, ask students to share their lists aloud with a partner or the class. Keep the Prove It! lists to put in a class word bank or chart for future reference.

NOTE Some students might identify adjectives that form the comparative and superlative differently. As appropriate, discuss that the comparative forms of some two-syllable adjectives and all three-syllable adjectives use the words *more* and *most*: for example, *more generous* and *most generous*.

Day 4

Spelling for Writing

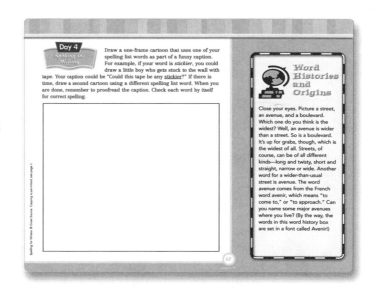

Have students use one of their spelling list words to draw a one-frame cartoon that uses the word as part of a caption. Remind students that the caption must be associated with their drawing. If students are done with their first drawing before time is up, have them draw another cartoon using a second spelling list word.

Remind students to:

- reread what they have written to see if it makes sense and complies with the directions for the activity.

- check the spelling of word list words and all other words.

- use punctuation correctly and effectively to convey the message or humor of the cartoon.

Proofreading Tip Remind students of the ways that they can slow their reading pace for careful proofreading: read aloud, touch a pencil point to each letter.

WORD HISTORY Share the origin of *boulevard* with students. The word *boulevard* comes from French. It originally referred to "the horizontal section of a rampart" or "a promenade." However, in the seventeenth century, the word acquired the meaning of "a broad street lined with trees." It was this meaning that was adopted in English. In some areas of the United States, *boulevard* has the additional meaning of "a grassed or landscaped strip in the center of the road or between the curbing and sidewalks."

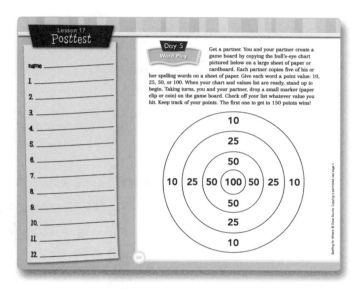

Word Play and Posttest

Have students play a game of "Bull's Eye" with their words. Have students find a partner and together copy the game board onto a large sheet of paper or cardboard. The center ring is worth 100 points. The second ring is worth 50 points. The third ring is worth 25 points. The outer ring is worth 10 points. Have students choose five of their spelling words and assign values for each on a separate sheet of paper. Students then drop a marker (paper clip or coin) onto the game board to see where it lands. Students check off whatever value the marker hits. The first student to reach 150 points wins! (Save the bull's eyes for future games.)

Posttest Have students tear out the perforated posttest. Students should pair up with their buddies or partners and exchange School Lists (page 65 in the Student Book). Students take turns testing each other on their respective spelling words. Collect the posttest sheets and record the correct response percentages. Mastery is 10 out of 12 words correct, or 80%. For students who do not achieve posttest mastery, see page xv in this Teacher's Edition.

After the posttest, have students select one or two anchor words to help them remember the word feature in this lesson. Record the words on the "Anchor Words" poster and refer to them in the Review lesson.

Lesson 18

Homonyms. These are words that sound the same but are spelled differently and have different meanings (*wear, where*).

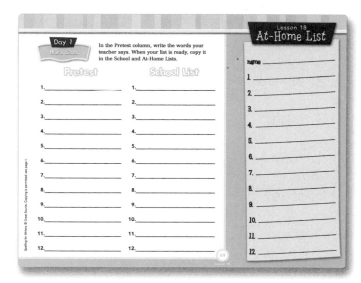

Day 1
Pretest and Word Lists

Before Photocopy the Answer Key/ Shopping List page (page 86 in this Teacher's Edition) for each student.

During Say each word in bold, read the context sentence, and repeat the word. Have students record the pretest words in the pretest column on page 69 of the Student Book.

After Distribute to students a copy of the Answer Key/Shopping List page so that they can correct their pretests.

- Students should cross out any misspelled words and write the correct spelling. If one word is misspelled, consider the pair incorrect. Word pairs that were correctly spelled can be replaced with word pairs from the Shopping List.

- Be sure that each student has a list of six word pairs, which they should copy into the School and At-Home Lists and the Sorting Boxes (page 86).

Pretest context sentences (spelling word in bold)

1. We are not allowed to **wear** hats in school.
2. **Where** do you go to school?
3. What is the **main** idea of this story?
4. The horse's long **mane** was golden brown.
5. **Steel** is made by combining iron and carbon.
6. The thief will try to **steal** the diamond ring.
7. A scale measures **weight**.
8. I hate to **wait** for the bus on cold mornings.
9. The **creek** is home to many frogs.
10. The old wood floors **creak** when I walk on them.
11. May I have a **piece** of pie, please?
12. The opposite of war is **peace**.

At-Home List Send the At-Home List home so that families can use the following activities with heir students: parts of speech sort, homonym words sentence.

> NOTE The Shopping List provides words below grade level (the first two rows), at grade level (the middle two rows), and above grade level (the last two rows) that still use the feature (homonyms).

Name _____

Answer Key

1. wear   7. weight

2. where   8. wait

3. main   9. creek

4. mane   10. creak

5. steel   11. piece

6. steal   12. peace

Shopping List

hear	there	way	cent
here	their	weigh	scent
lead	need	wring	beat
led	knead	ring	beet
pray	vane	stake	haul
prey	vain	steak	hall

Sorting Boxes

Day 2
Word Sorting

Have students look at the words carefully and decide for themselves a way or ways in which they can sort the words (do an open sort). Once they have made their sorts, have them write a generalization about the words. How students think about the words shows you what they understand about them.

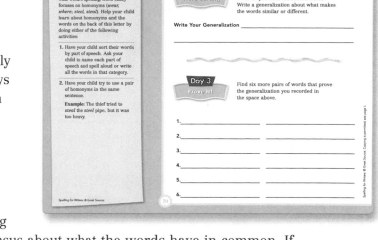

- After students do an open sort, bring the class together to come to consensus about what the words have in common. If students have not or cannot come to consensus, model a way to sort all the words. You can use oversized word cards (CD-ROM) or a cut-up transparency (Transparency 18) and overhead for the demonstration.

- Show homonym pairs (*wear/where, piece/peace*). Have students pronounce each word in the pair. Ask students what is the same about the words. Ask how the words differ. Then have students work independently to make homonym pairs.

- Ask volunteers to make a statement about how their words were sorted: *Some words sound the same, but they have different spellings and meanings.*

- Have students write the generalization in their Student Book (page 70). You might also write the generalization on a sentence strip or poster to display for the duration of the lesson. Leave room for students to add some of their Prove It! words from Day 3.

- Have students store their Sorting Boxes. (See page xi in this Teacher's Edition.)

Day 3
Prove It!

Students should review the generalization from Day 2: *Some words may sound the same, but they have different spellings and meanings.* Then send them off to find in readable materials more examples that prove the generalization to be true. (They should look for pairs of words.) Tell students that they must be able to read and pronounce any word they find and record for the activity. Adjust the amount and kind of reading material students will use and the number of words they should find, according to their needs. Keep the Prove It! lists to put in a class word bank or chart for future reference.

NOTE Students looking for a challenge might want to look for homonyms that have three spellings, such as *rain/rein/reign, to/too/two, for/four/fore,* or *their/there/they're.*

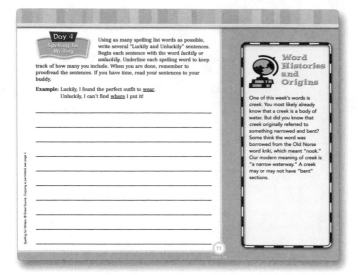

Have students use as many spelling list homonym pairs as possible to write "Luckily and Unluckily" sentences, as described in the Student Book. Remind students that their first sentence must begin with the word *luckily* and their second sentence must begin with *unluckily*. Students should underline their spelling words to help them keep track of how many they are able to include. Share the example from the Student Book as a model:

Example: Luckily, I found the perfect outfit to *wear*.
Unluckily, I can't find *where* I put it!

Share these tips with students:

- Reread what you have written to see if it makes sense and complies with the directions for the activity (sometimes there is more than one step to follow).

- Look for word omissions (sometimes the brain gets ahead of the hand!).

- Check punctuation and capitalization.

- Tally the number of spelling list words included; can you add more?

Proofreading Tip Tell students that careful proofreaders check for one item at a time, which means that they have to read through a piece of writing several times. Suggest that students check their captions once for spelling and once for proper sentence structure (capital letters, end punctuation).

WORD HISTORY Discuss the onomatopoeic features of *creak*. Explain to students that onomatopoeia words sound like what they mean. For example, in the sentence "Old doors always creak when I open them," the word *creak* is a sound-effects word that refers to the sound of the doors. Have students suggest other onomatopoeia words. (Suggestions may include *bang, clank, hiss, buzz, hum, cuckoo, splash, slap*.)

Day 5

Word Play and Posttest

Have students try to make up some riddles using their homonyms pairs and the riddle tips. When students finish writing their riddles, have them trade riddles with their partner. Each partner tries to answer the riddle. Walk students through the tips and the model offered on Student Book page 72 and below.

"Crack Up" Riddles Tips

1. Find words that sound alike.
   Example: *peace* and *piece*
2. Think of a sentence or phrase in which either word makes sense.
   Example: He just wants a little *peace* (*piece*).
3. Ask yourself questions:
   Who might want a little peace? (a teacher around lots of noise)
   Who might want a little piece? (a kid being served something yucky)
4. Create a riddle question with this pattern: Why is a ___ like a ___?
   Sample Riddle: Why is a teacher with noisy students like a boy being served spinach pie?

Posttest Have students tear out the perforated posttest. Students should pair up with their buddies or partners and exchange School Lists (page 69 in the Student Book). Students take turns testing each other on their respective spelling words. Collect the posttest sheets and record the correct response percentages. Mastery is 10 out of 12 words correct, or 80%. For students who do not achieve posttest mastery, see page xv in this Teacher's Edition.

After the posttest, have students select one or two anchor words to help them remember the word feature in this lesson. Record the words on the "Anchor Words" poster and refer to them in the Review lesson.

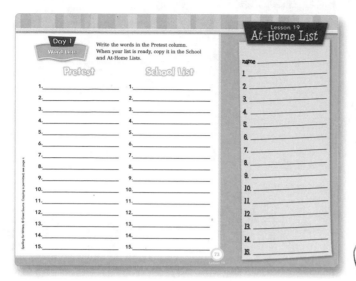

Day 1
Pretest and
Word Lists

Before There are three options for selecting the pretest words. Choose the one most appropriate for your students.

1. Have students think of words that fit the spelling patterns and write them.

2. Use the words that you and your class collected on the "Anchor Words" poster.

3. Use the examples given below.

If you will dictate the words, either from the "Anchor Words" poster or from below, write them on a copy of Copy Master 1. Photocopy the filled-in answer key page for each student.

During Announce each word feature. Then state the spelling generalization and give the words or tell students to think of their own words. Students will write one pretest word for each feature on page 73 of the Student Book.

After If you dictated the words, distribute a copy of the answer key so that students can self-correct their pretests. Otherwise, correct students' pretests.

• For any word features that students got correct, they can go back to the lesson for that feature and select from their Prove It! list a word they want to learn to spell.

• Be sure that each student has a list of correctly spelled words, which they should copy into the School and At-Home Lists and the Sorting Boxes (use Copy Master 1 for the Sorting Boxes).

Word Features and Generalizations

1. **Short Vowels.** Every word in English has at least one vowel phoneme. These words have short vowel sounds: *access, kept, drizzle, odd,* and *luck.* (*Lessons 2 and 3*)

2. **Long Vowels (final *y*).** When a long vowel sound comes at the end of a word or syllable, it probably ends in *y* (*supply*) or a vowel plus *y* (*repay*). (*Lesson 4*)

3. **Long Vowels (*e* marker, silent letter patterns).** When a word ends with a silent *e,* the vowel closest to the silent *e* represents a long vowel sound. Examples are *fade, shine,* and *globe.* Sometimes vowel letters make a pattern in which one vowel is long and one is silent, as in *beast, float, paint,* and *elbow.* (*Lessons 5 and 6*)

4. **Silent Consonant Patterns.** Consonant letters can make a pattern in which one is silent, for example *tomb, knife,* and *gnaw*. (*Lesson 7*)

5. *R*-**Controlled Vowels.** When *r* follows a vowel, the *r* influences, or controls, the vowel sound. Examples are *pillar, germs, thirty,* and *motor*. (*Lesson 8*)

6. **Diphthongs.** Two side-by-side vowels can represent a sound that is neither short nor long. Examples are *moist, gown, loyal,* and *pound*. (*Lesson 9*)

7. **Plurals *(-s, -es, y to i).*** Add *–s* to form the plural of most words (*rockets*). Add *–es* to words that end with *ch, x, s,* or *sh* (*arches*). Change *y* to *i* before adding *–es* (*berries*). (*Lesson 10*)

8. **Past Tense.** The past-tense verbs in this lesson represent three sounds but only two spellings (*kept, whined, supported*). (*Lesson 11*)

9. **Compound Words.** A compound word is made by putting two words together: *background, whenever,* and *storybook*. (*Lesson 12*)

10. **Doubled Consonants (before endings).** When the base word has one short vowel sound and ends in a consonant, the consonant is doubled before adding the ending or suffix *(skipped, tagging)*. (*Lesson 13*)

11. **Prefixes and Suffixes.** When a prefix or suffix is added to a word, the meaning of the word changes (*unable, playful*). (*Lesson 14*)

12. **Derivations and Relations.** Words that are related may sound different but are similar in spelling (*reduce/reduction*). (*Lesson 15*)

13. **Consonant Blends.** When a consonant comes before *l* or *r*, the sounds are blended together (*blade, grapes*). (*Lesson 16*)

14. **Comparatives and Superlatives.** Endings are added to words to show comparison of different numbers of objects. Sometimes a spelling change is required (*louder, busiest*). (*Lesson 17*)

15. **Homonyms.** These are words that sound the same but are spelled differently and have different meanings (*wear, where*). (*Lesson 18*)

At-Home List Send the At-Home List home so that families can use the following activities with their children: word sorting, word hunt, word-guessing game.

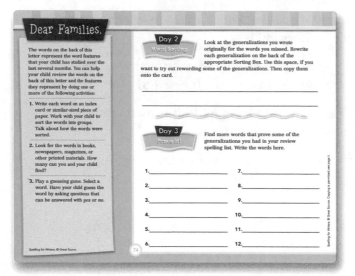

Students work with partners to revisit the generalizations for words they misspelled on the Pretest. Suggest that they look back at the generalizations they wrote in their book at time of initial study of the lesson's words. Tell them to try to reword the generalizations to help them better remember them. Even students who got all the words correct can revisit and reword several generalizations that were unclear to them the first time.

The rewording process should provide students insight into what "rules" govern many different sets of words. Students should rewrite their revised generalizations on the backs of their Sorting Boxes. (Make a photocopy of Copy Master 1, blank Sorting Boxes, for students to use).

As a closing step, have students work in pairs to sort their words into groups that make sense. Circulate through the room to talk with students about their word sorts. Students' explanations of their sorts tells you what they understand about how words work.

After students revisit and revise the several generalizations for this lesson's review, send them off to find in readable materials more examples that prove as many of the generalizations as possible to be true. Tell students that they must be able to

read and pronounce any word they find and record for the activity. Adjust the amount and kind of reading material students will use, according to their needs. Keep the Prove It! lists to put in a class word bank or chart for future reference.

Day 4
Spelling for Writing

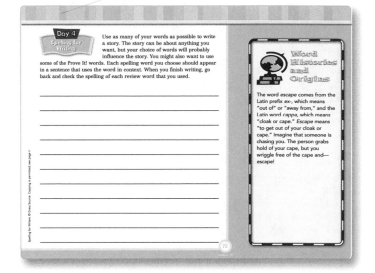

Day 4 Spelling for Writing

Use as many of your words as possible to write a story. The story can be about anything you want, but your choice of words will probably influence the story. You might also want to use some of the Prove It! words. Each spelling word you choose should appear in a sentence that uses the word in context. When you finish writing, go back and check the spelling of each review word that you used.

Word Histories and Origins

The word *escape* comes from the Latin prefix *ex-*, which means "out of" or "away from," and the Latin word *cappa*, which means "cloak or cape." *Escape* means "to get out of your cloak or cape." Imagine that someone is chasing you. The person grabs hold of your cape, but you wriggle free of the cape and— escape!

Tell students to look at their list of spelling words and use as many of them as possible to write a story. Sentences should be constructed carefully so that words are explained in context.

Tell students that

- the words they choose will help determine the content of their stories.

- all stories have a beginning, a middle, and an ending.

- dialogue helps the reader know what the characters are like and adds interest to the story.

- the sentences that contain spelling words must clearly convey the meaning of each spelling word used.

Proofreading Tip Remind students once again that reading and proofreading are different. Ask students to share which proofreading strategies they use and which ones are most helpful. Some of the strategies they might mention are the following: read for one item at a time, touch each word with a pencil point, read the words aloud, look for errors the writer commonly makes, and work with a partner.

Word Histories and Origins Students are told about the origin of the word *escape*, which means "to get out of your cape." Encourage students to look up the origins of words that pique their interest. Some resources for word histories and origins are listed on Teacher's Edition page 186.

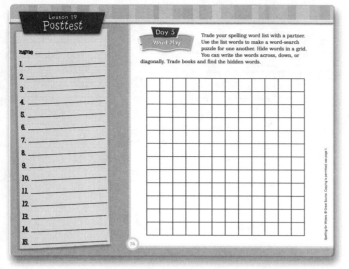

Have students swap spelling lists and
create a word find for each other. Words
should be hidden in a grid and can be
placed so they can be read horizontally,
vertically, or diagonally. Once the words
are in place, students should fill the grid
with random letters that do not form
words. Once the word searches are
ready, have the partners trade books and
find the hidden words.

Other activities that students can do to review the words include the following:

• Have students choose a set of Sorting Boxes from a previous week and time themselves when they sort the cards. Students should sort them several times to see
whether their sorting time gets faster. (Copy Masters of the pretest words can be
found in the Transparencies and Copy Masters folder. Or, generate word cards from
the CD-ROM.)

• Students can use their review list to play one of the Word Play games from a previous lesson: for example, "Hangman," "Hit or Miss," or "Bull's Eye." They could also
make a crossword puzzle.

• Generate a practice activity from the CD-ROM.

Posttest Have students carefully tear out the posttest form on the Student Book
page 76. Students should pair up with their buddies or partners and exchange School
Lists (page 74 in the Student Book). Students take turns testing each other on their
respective spelling words. Mastery is 80% of the number of words they had for the
week (12 correct out of 15). For students who do not achieve posttest mastery, see page
xi in this Teacher's Edition.

Lesson 20   Benchmark Assessment

Days 1-2
Word Lists

Before Have students turn to page 77 in the Student Book, where they will record the spelling words.

During Say each word in boldface (page 96) aloud. The word features in parentheses are for your information only. These words were specifically chosen because they represent grade level words for that feature. If you substituted any other words, in Lesson 1, use them here. It is recommended that this assessment be administered over two to five days, in short intervals, in order to best meet the needs of your students and to avoid student fatigue. On Days 3-5, if the assessment is still ongoing, students can continue with the other activities after you administer a small portion of the assessment.

After Interpret students' responses, analyzing first their successes in spelling a word that meets the word feature criterion and then taking a hard look at where they may have miscued, perhaps recalling a different word feature and misapplying it. We suggest you do not mark in the Student Book. A record sheet is provided (see page 179 in this Teacher's Edition). This records the features and allows you to document growth for each student. It is important for students not to see the markings, so simply transfer any attempts to the record sheet. This reinforces the understanding that *Spelling for Writers* developmentally supports the spelling strategies that students bring to their writing, rather than focusing on mastery of whole words. As you will notice, the students' profile easily documents growth.

Days 1-2
Word Lists

In the columns, write the words your teacher says.

Benchmark Assessment

1._____ 13._____
2._____ 14._____
3._____ 15._____
4._____ 16._____
5._____ 17._____
6._____ 18._____
7._____ 19._____
8._____ 20._____
9._____ 21._____
10._____ 22._____
11._____ 23._____
12._____ 24._____

77

Dear Families,

Your child has taken one of three benchmark assessments in the spelling program, *Spelling for Writers*. The purpose of the assessments is to provide an overall picture of students' developing knowledge of the word features (patterns and structures of words) that will be taught this year.

Benchmark assessments are administered in lessons 1, 20, and 36 of *Spelling for Writers*. The benchmark words were carefully selected to reflect each child's current knowledge of certain word features. Mastery is not expected and grades are not given. Rather, the benchmark assessments are a tool for planning instruction.

(continued)

Benchmark Assessment The Benchmark Assessment occurs in Lessons 1, 20, and 36 to measure students' growth and development in spelling across the year. The same words must be used each time in order to have a consistent way to measure students' growth on each feature.

1. **acid** (short vowel)
2. **button** (short vowel in 2-syllable words)
3. **angry** (long vowels, final *y*)
4. **chase** (*e* marker)
5. **mule** (*e* marker)
6. **close** (*e* marker)
7. **dime** (*e* marker)
8. **Pete** (*e* marker)
9. **avenue** (long vowels, silent letter pattern)
10. **doubtful** (consonant, silent letter pattern)
11. **southerner** (*r*-controlled vowels)
12. **snowbound** (diphthong)
13. **studios** (plurals)
14. **done** (irregular past-tense)
15. **withhold** (compound words)
16. **wrapping** (doubling before ending or suffix)
17. **uncommon** (prefix)

18. **painless** (suffix)
19. **angel/angelic** (derivations and relations)
20. **slammed** (blends)
21. **lovelier/loveliest** (comparatives)
22. **threw/through** (homonyms)
23. **taught** (complex vowel pattern)
24. **launch** (preconsonant nasals)
25. **knee/knelt** (vowel alternations)
26. **accurate** (doubling at syllable juncture)
27. **odor** (*r*-controlled in more complex words)
28. **incorrect** (prefixes and meanings)
29. **connect** (doubling at juncture)
30. **undoable** (prefix/suffix in the same word)
31. **oxen** (irregular plurals)
32. **shoreline** (compound words)
33. **missed/mist** (homonyms)
34. **wouldn't** (contractions)

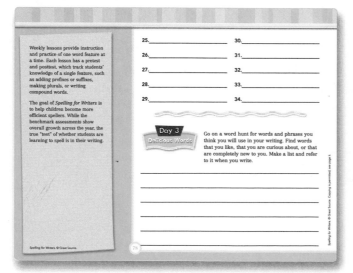

Letter to the Families

On pages 77-78 of the Student Book, there is a letter addressed to your students' families. The letter explains in a brief way the purpose of benchmark assessments: examining the student's responses enables you to measure the student's knowledge of word features studied this year, a prerequisite for expanding the student's spelling strategies. Please take time to read the letter. It will help you understand our approach to spelling and word study.

Day 3

Delicious Words

If students are still taking the benchmark assessment, administer more of the words before students begin the word-hunt activity.

Rather than sending students on a hunt for words that exemplify a particular word feature, send them off to find "delicious" words that they can use to enhance their writing. The words can be single or in phrases, completely unknown words, or words students would like to find out more about.

Once students have collected words in their individual lists, have them each select one or two words to share with the class. Words that the class especially likes can be listed on the "Delicious Words" poster as a resource of terrific words to be used in writing. Words that are on display in the classroom should always be spelled correctly!

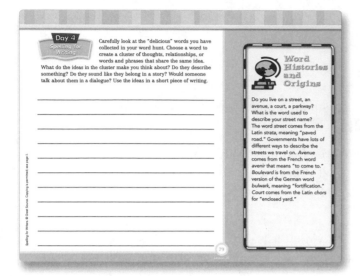

An effective strategy for planning writing is clustering. Clustering allows writers to think freely and web ideas around an interesting word. Students should use a separate sheet of paper to make their clusters (word webs) and then do their writing on Student Book page 79. Encourage students to choose a word from the word hunt to cluster thoughts, relationships, and phrases associated with the word. Tell students to let the ideas in the cluster determine what they will write about, whether it is a description, a short story, or a dialogue.

Offer students these tips for writing:

- A description uses sensory words that make the reader see, hear, feel, taste, or smell what the writer is describing.

- A short story has a beginning, middle, and end. It also has characters and a setting.

- A dialogue should sound natural, as if the people are really talking. Quotation marks show the words uttered by the speakers.

Proofreading Tip Remind students that a careful proofreader checks for one item at a time, which means that students should make several passes through their writing.

Word History We use street names all the time, but where did the names originate? The word history on Student Book page 79 explains where some of the words for *street* came from. On Student Book page 80, students are asked to look at a local map to find out what the streets are called. Are there *roads*, *drives*, or *ways* in your town? Students are also asked to find out how some of the streets got their names. Sometimes the history of a street name will yield some insight into the history of the town.

Day 5
Word Play

Your students have been asked to choose a word from the word hunt, one of the "delicious" words, and describe it without using the specific word. They must write several clues so that their partner may guess which word is being described. Students should complete the first two rows of the word chart and then trade charts with their partner. The game can be continued on separate sheets of paper.

Find the Story

Be a word historian!

Get a map of your city and see what the streets are called. Collect some interesting street names. How do you think the city planners chose these names?

_____
_____
_____
_____
_____
_____
_____
_____
_____

Day 5
Word Play

Choose a word from the word hunt and describe it without using the actual word. First, choose four "delicious" words to put into the Word Bank in the chart below. Then write clues for one of them. Have your partner read the clues and select the word he or she thinks you have described.

Word Bank
Clues
Which word is it?

Lesson 21 Complex Vowel Patterns.
Two vowels together can stand for a vowel sound that is neither short nor long (appl*au*d, f*ou*ght, cr*aw*l).

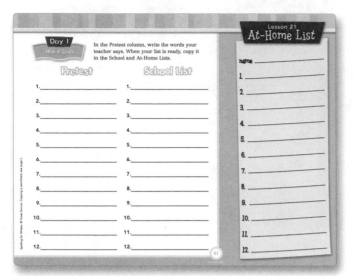

Day 1
Pretest and Word Lists

Before Photocopy the Answer Key/ Shopping List page (page 101 in this Teacher's Edition) for each student.

During Say each word in bold, read the context sentence, and repeat the word. Have students record the pretest words in the pretest column on page 81 of the Student Book.

After Distribute to students a copy of the Answer Key/Shopping List page so that they can correct their pretests.

- Students should cross out any misspelled words and write the correct spelling. Words that were correctly spelled can be replaced with words from the Shopping List. Identify the list from which students should choose their words. (See below.)

- Be sure that each student has a list of twelve correctly spelled words, which they should copy into the School and At-Home Lists and the Sorting Boxes (page 101).

Pretest context sentences (spelling word in bold)

1. At the end of a show, the audience members usually **applaud**.
2. The boxer **fought** the heavyweight champion.
3. Dad **caught** a huge fish with his new fishing rod!
4. My mom's **daughter** is also my sister.
5. The artist created a beautiful **drawing**.
6. Please use **caution** in handling that hot dish.
7. The **author** just published her second book.
8. The tomato **sauce** on the meatballs was delicious.
9. Babies **crawl** before they begin to walk.
10. I hate to see the days get shorter during **autumn**.
11. The roller-coaster ride was **awesome**!
12. When I am tired, I **yawn** a lot.

At-Home List Send the At-Home List home so that families can use the following activities with their students: meaning clues, missing vowels.

> **NOTE** The Shopping List provides words below grade level (the first two rows), at grade level (the middle two rows), and above grade level (the last two rows).

Name _____

Answer Key

1. applaud   7. author

2. fought   8. sauce

3. caught   9. crawl

4. daughter   10. autumn

5. drawing   11. awesome

6. caution   12. yawn

Shopping List

jaw	cause	dawn	taught
because	bought	laundry	launch
claw	thoughtful	pause	hawk
auction	clause	spawn	crawling
applause	brawny	authority	staunch
awful	trough	caulk	causeway

Sorting Boxes

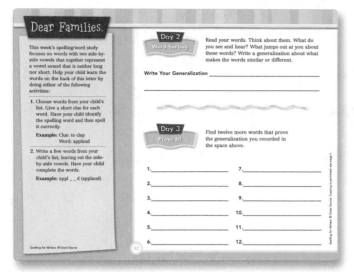

Have students look at the words carefully and decide for themselves a way or ways in which they can sort the words (do an open sort). Once they have made their sorts, have them write a generalization about the words. How students think about the words shows you what they understand about them. The written generalization is evidence of their thought process.

• After students do an open sort, bring the class together to come to consensus. If students have not or cannot come to consensus, model for them a way to sort using all the words. You can use oversized word cards (CD-ROM) or a cut-up transparency (Transparency 19) and overhead to facilitate your model.

• The three general categories for the sorting should be words with *au*, *ou*, and *aw*. After students successfully make their sorts, guide them to notice the one sound that the side-by-side vowels represent.

• Model for students how to make a statement about how all their words were sorted: *Two side-by-side vowels can represent a vowel sound that is neither long nor short.*

• Have students write the generalization in their Student Book (page 82). You might also write the generalization on a sentence strip or poster to display for the duration of the lesson. Leave room for students to add some of their Prove It! words from Day 3.

• Have students store their Sorting Boxes. (See page xi in this Teacher's Edition.)

Students should review the generalization: *Sometimes two side-by-side vowels can represent a vowel sound that is neither long nor short.* Then send them off to find in readable materials more examples that prove the generalization to be true. Tell students that they must be able to read and pronounce any word they find and record for the activity. Adjust the amount and kind of reading material students will use and the number of words they should find, according to their needs. To expose each student to more words, ask students to share their lists aloud with a partner or the class. Keep the Prove It! lists to put in a class word bank or chart for future reference.

Day 3

Prove It!

Day 4
Spelling for Writing

The goal of any spelling program is for students to be able to use their words in writing. Have students write a cinquain poem using at least two of their spelling list words. Review the cinquain poem's special features. Students should underline their spelling words.

Remind students of the elements of a cinquain poem:

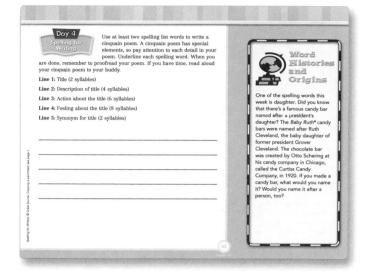

Line 1:	Title	2 syllables
Line 2:	Description of title	4 syllables
Line 3:	Action about the title	6 syllables
Line 4:	Feeling about the title	8 syllables
Line 5:	Synonym for title	2 syllables

Proofreading Tip Suggest that students use the proofreading strategy of reading aloud. This will help slow students' reading rate so that they can check each word individually. Students can whisper so as not to disturb their neighbors.

WORD HISTORY Students may enjoy knowing the origin of another well-known candy—Lifesavers®. In 1912, Clarence Crane, a candy maker in Cleveland, Ohio, found that summer was a bad time to sell chocolate because it kept melting. So, to improve candy sales, he made a hard confection that stayed fresh no matter how hot it was. There were other mints at the time, so Crane thought he would make his mints different by putting a hole in the middle of them. Since they resembled a life preserver, he called them Lifesavers!

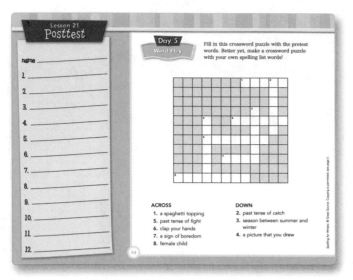

name _____

1. _____
2. _____
3. _____
4. _____
5. _____
6. _____
7. _____
8. _____
9. _____
10. _____
11. _____
12. _____

Day 5
Word Play

Fill in this crossword puzzle with the pretest words. Better yet, make a crossword puzzle with your own spelling list words!

ACROSS
1. a spaghetti topping
5. past tense of fight
6. clap your hands
7. a sign of boredom
8. female child

DOWN
2. past tense of catch
3. season between summer and winter
4. a picture that you drew

Students will fill in the crossword puzzle with the pretest words. Students who need extra support can work with a spelling buddy to complete the crossword puzzle. Students who need to be challenged should be encouraged to make their own crossword puzzles, using their spelling list words. Graph paper is useful for creating a puzzle. Place copies of the student-made puzzles in the word center, or keep them accessible for students to do during free time.

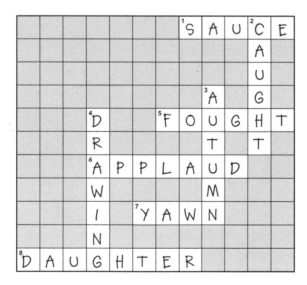

Posttest Have students tear out the perforated posttest. Students should pair up with their buddies or partners and exchange School Lists (page 81 in the Student Book). Students take turns testing each other on their respective spelling words. Collect the posttest sheets and record the correct response percentages. Mastery is 10 out of 12 words correct, or 80%. For students who do not achieve posttest mastery, see page xv in this Teacher's Edition. After the posttest, have students select one or two anchor words to help them remember the word feature in this lesson. Record the words on the "Anchor Words" poster and refer to them in the Review lesson.

Periodically, check writing samples from your students for transfer of the word features that have been taught. The features for the last three lessons follow:

Lesson 17: Comparatives and Superlatives
Lesson 18: Homonyms
Lesson 21: Complex Vowel Patterns

Lesson 22 Preconsonant Nasals.
The letters *m* and *n* are nasal consonants. When they come before another consonant, they are called preconsonant nasals, as in *chomp* and *belong*.

Day 1
Pretest and Word Lists

Before Photocopy the Answer Key/ Shopping List page (page 106 in this Teacher's Edition) for each student.

During Say each word in bold, read the context sentence, and repeat the word. Have students record the pretest words in the pretest column on page 85 of the Student Book.

After Distribute to students a copy of the Answer Key/Shopping List page so that they can correct their pretests.

- Students should cross out any misspelled words and write the correct spelling. Words that were correctly spelled can be replaced with words from the Shopping List. Identify the list from which students should choose their words. (See below.)

- Be sure that each student has a list of twelve correctly spelled words, which they should copy into the School and At-Home Lists and the Sorting Boxes (page 106).

Pretest context sentences (spelling word in bold)

1. After his last fight, the heavyweight **champ** retired.
2. The hungry dog will **chomp** on his toy bones.
3. That hat and scarf **belong** to Kyle.
4. Rotten cheese sure does **stink**!
5. Are there any **vacant** rooms in this hotel?
6. The door **sprung** open suddenly.
7. The **chipmunk** gathers food for the winter.
8. I love seafood, especially **shrimp**.
9. For April Fools, I will play a **prank** on my brother.
10. You should call 911 for **urgent** problems only.
11. The **skunk** releases a strong odor in self-defense.
12. When writing, you should always **indent** a new paragraph.

At-Home List Send the At-Home List home so that families can use the following activities with their students: letter fill-ins, rhyming sentences.

> NOTE The Shopping List provides words below grade level (the first two rows), at grade level (the middle two rows), and above grade level (the last two rows).

Name _____

Answer Key

1. champ
2. chomp
3. belong
4. stink
5. vacant
6. sprung
7. chipmunk
8. shrimp
9. prank
10. urgent
11. skunk
12. indent

Shopping List

| camp | blind | dump | plunked |
| trunk | print | along | jump |

| plump | stamp | shrank | string |
| agent | blank | paint | swamp |

| blonde | enchant | vibrant | servant |
| plank | oblong | trump | skimpy |

Sorting Boxes

Day 2
Word Sorting

Encourage students to read their word lists and think about the words, looking for generalizations that they can make about how the words are similar or different. Have students sort their words, which shows you what they understand about them. The written generalization is evidence of their thought process.

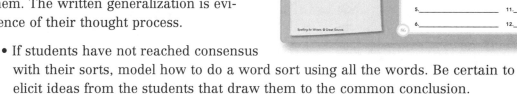

- If students have not reached consensus with their sorts, model how to do a word sort using all the words. Be certain to elicit ideas from the students that draw them to the common conclusion.

- Guide students to discover that all the words in this lesson have a two-letter consonant pattern in which the first of the two letters is hard to hear clearly because the sound it represents is nasal when pronounced.

- You can use oversized word cards (CD-ROM) or a cut-up transparency (Transparency 20) and overhead to facilitate your model. The two general categories for the sort should be words with preconsonant *m* and words with preconsonant *n*.

- Focus on the words *jump* and *pink*. Ask students to pronounce the words with you. Help them notice how the *m* and *n*, respectively, fade in comparison to the final consonant *p* and *k*. You may see students leaving the "hard to hear" sound out of their spelling. Students need to be encouraged to use their "spelling eyes" to examine these words.

- Identify *m* and *n* as nasal sounds, or sounds produced when the air is blocked in the oral cavity but escapes through the nose. Have students hold their nose and try saying the word to demonstrate the nasal sound. (When the nasal sound comes before another consonant it is called "preconsonant.")

- Model for students how to make a statement about how all their words were sorted: *When* m *and* n *come before another consonant letter, their nasal sounds are hard to hear.*

- Have students write the generalization in their Student Book (page 86). You might also write the generalization on a sentence strip or poster to display for the duration of the lesson. Leave room for students to add some of their Prove It! words from Day 3.

- Have students store their Sorting Boxes. (See page xi in this Teacher's Edition.)

Students should review the generalization from Day 2: *When* m *and* n *come before another consonant letter, their nasal sounds are hard to hear.* Then send them off to find in readable materials more examples that prove the generalization to be true. Tell students that they must be able to read and pronounce any word they find and record for the activity. Adjust the amount and kind of reading material students will use and the number of words they must find, according to their needs. Keep the Prove It! lists to put in a class word bank or chart for future reference.

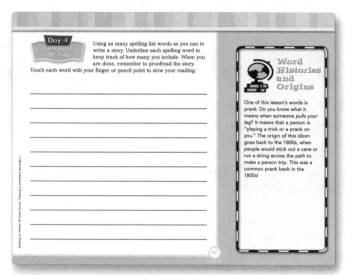

Day 4

Spelling for Writing

The goal of any spelling program is for students to be able to use their words in writing. Have students use as many spelling list words as possible to write a story. Students should underline their spelling words to help them keep track of how many they are able to include.

Share these tips with students:

• Reread what you have written to see if it makes sense.

• The story should have characters, a setting, and events (at least one big event).

• The ending should pull the story together.

Proofreading Tip Most spelling errors can be caught if students take their time. Advise students to point to each word with a finger or pencil point, which will force them to look at each word individually. They should say or whisper each spelling word because their mouth position will give them a clue as to whether the nasal sound is represented by *m* (lips together) or *n* (tongue on top of mouth).

WORD HISTORY One of the preconsonant nasal words is *shrimp.* Ask students if they know any dishes that have shrimp in them. Make a list of students' responses. Add *gumbo* if needed. Tell students that gumbo is a stew or soup made with okra, chicken, seafood, and vegetables. The origin of the word *gumbo* is African. In Unbbundu the word is *ochinggombo* and in Luba (a tribal group in Congo, Zaire) the word is *chinggombo,* both meaning "okra"—which is one of the main ingredients of the dish.

Day 5
Word Play and Posttest

Students will experiment with adding endings to their spelling words. Have them copy at least six of their spelling words. Next to each word, they should write related words, words to which prefixes, suffixes, or inflections have been added. Some words will generate more related words than others, but have students share their lists with each other so that everyone has an opportunity to hear or read a lot of different words.

Example: champ—champion, championship, champs

Posttest Have students tear out the perforated posttest. Students should pair up with their buddies or partners and exchange School Lists (page 85 in the Student Book). Students take turns testing each other on their respective spelling words. Collect the posttest sheets and record the correct response percentages. Mastery is 10 out of 12 words correct, or 80%. For students who do not achieve posttest mastery, see page xv in this Teacher's Edition.

After the posttest, have students select one or two anchor words to help them remember the word feature in this lesson. Record the words on the "Anchor Words" poster and refer to them in the Review lesson.

Lesson 22
Posttest

name _____
1. _____
2. _____
3. _____
4. _____
5. _____
6. _____
7. _____
8. _____
9. _____
10. _____
11. _____
12. _____

88

Day 5
Word Play

Use your spelling words to make more words. Write six of your words on the lines below. Then think about beginnings or endings you can add to each word. For example, if one of your words is *vacant*, you could write *vacantly*. Write the new words.

_____
_____
_____
_____
_____
_____

Lesson 23

Vowel Alternations. When an ending is added to a word, the vowel sound can change, although the spelling is preserved, as in *wide* and *width*.

Day 1
Pretest and Word Lists

Before Photocopy the Answer Key/Shopping List page (page 111 in this Teacher's Edition) for each student.

During Say each word in bold, read the context sentence, and repeat the word. Have students record the pretest words in the pretest column on page 89 of the Student Book.

After Distribute to students a copy of the Answer Key/Shopping List page so that they can correct their pretests.

- Students should cross out any misspelled words and write the correct spelling. If one word is misspelled, consider the pair incorrect. Word pairs that were correctly spelled can be replaced with word pairs from the Shopping List.

- Be sure that each student has a list of twelve correctly spelled words, which they should copy into the School and At-Home Lists and the Sorting Boxes (page 111).

Pretest context sentences (spelling word in bold)

1. The bookstore has a *central* location in the mall.
2. The *centrality* of the location helps business.
3. The president will *declare* his candidacy for reelection.
4. The exact wording of his *declaration* is unknown.
5. The rectangle is 9 inches *wide*.
6. The *width* of the rectangle is 9 inches.
7. I will *invite* Jim to the surprise party.
8. Here is Jim's *invitation* to the party.
19. When you *divide* 8 by 4, you get 2.
10. In 8 divided by 4, the numeral 8 is the *dividend*.
11. The plumber will *install* new bathroom pipes.
12. How much will the pipe *installation* cost?

At-Home List Send the At-Home List home so that families can use the following activities with their students: black and blue, explanation of the generalization.

NOTE The Shopping List provides words below grade level (first two rows), at grade level (middle two rows), and above grade level (last two rows).

Name _____

Answer Key

1. central
2. centrality
3. declare
4. declaration
5. wide
6. width
7. invite
8. invitation
9. divide
10. dividend
11. install
12. installation

Shopping List

explain	reduce	comedy	product
explanation	reduction	comedian	production
ignite	nation	provide	total
ignition	national	provision	totality
major	define	editor	decide
majority	definition	editorial	decision

Sorting Boxes

Lesson 23

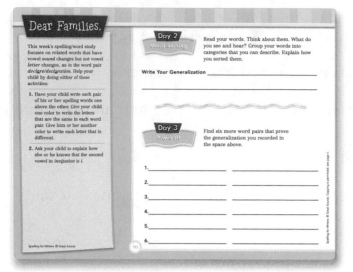

Day 2
Word Sorting

Encourage students to read their word lists and think about the words, looking for generalizations that they can make about how the words are similar or different. Have students sort their words, which shows you what they understand about them. The written generalization is evidence of their thought process.

- If students have not reached consensus with their sorting, model a way to sort, using all the words. Be certain to elicit ideas from the students that draw them to the common conclusion.

- Guide them to discover that a word to which a suffix has been added often has a vowel sound that is different from that in the base word; the letter that represents the vowel sound, however, does not change.

- You can use oversized word cards (CD-ROM) or a cut-up transparency (Transparency 21) and overhead to facilitate your model.

- First, model how to sort the words into related pairs. Have students align the cards, one above the other. Guide students to notice the similar spelling the word pairs have.

- Next, focus on the pronunciation of the related word pairs. Do another sort, this time grouping the word pairs according to the vowel letter that stays the same, despite having a different pronunciation. Guide students to notice that there is a sound change but *not* a spelling change.

- Explain that knowing these "alternative" sounds for the vowels in related words can help students spell other related words. If they know *angelic,* then they know that *angel* ends with *el,* not *le,* because we hear "gel." Students must use their brains, ears, and eyes in learning these words.

- Model for students how to make a statement about how all their words were sorted: *When an ending is added to a word, the vowel sound can change, although the spelling is preserved.*

- Have students write the generalization in their Student Book (page 90). You might also write the generalization on a sentence strip or poster to display for the duration of the lesson. Leave room for students to add some of their Prove It! words from Day 3.

- Have students store their Sorting Boxes. (See page xi in this Teacher's Edition.)

Day 3

Prove It!

Students should review the generalization: *When an ending is added to a word, the vowel sound can change, although the spelling is preserved.* Then send them off to find in readable materials more examples that prove the generalization to be true (six pairs of words that illustrate the generalization). Tell students that they must be able to read and pronounce any word they find and record for the activity. Adjust the amount and kind of reading material students will use, according to their needs. Keep the Prove It! lists to put in a class word bank or chart for future reference.

Day 4

Spelling for Writing

Have students use at least four spelling list words to write true or false statements. After students have finished writing their statements, they should trade statements with their partners. Partners need to respond to each statement using T for true and F for false. Review the example on Student Book page 91. Share the following tips with students:

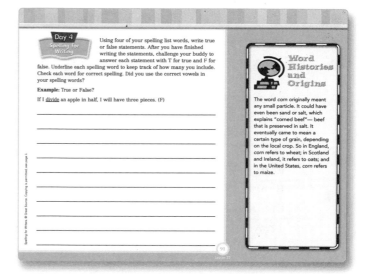

- Reread what you have written to see if it makes sense and complies with the directions for the activity.

- Look for any word omissions. (Sometimes the brain gets ahead of the hand!)

- Check capitalization and punctuation.

- Make sure your statements have an obvious true or false answer. (Make your statements factual not opinion-based).

Proofreading Tip Correct spelling is a courtesy from the writer to the reader. Suggest that students start with the last word in each sentence and continue toward the beginning of the sentence, considering each word individually.

WORD HISTORY Talk more with students about corn. Ask: What eats corn? Record students' responses. Add to the list *corn-weevil*. Explain that a weevil is a very destructive insect that feeds on different kinds of crops. The corn-weevil favors corn. The German word for corn-weevil was *hamastro.* Can students think of a small furry animal whose name sounds like *hamastro*? (hamster) Pose the question: Do you think hamsters eat corn?

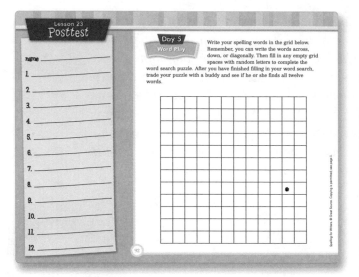

Each student will create a word-search puzzle that includes his or her spelling words. Students should write their words in the grid on Student Book page 92. Students can write their words across, down, or diagonally. Tell them to fill in any empty grid spaces with random letters. When the word-search puzzles are ready, have students trade with partners. Each partner finds and circles the hidden words. Students can refer to the Answer Key/Shopping List page if they need support in knowing what words to look for.

Posttest Have students tear out the perforated posttest. Students should pair up with their buddies or partners and exchange School Lists (page 89 in the Student Book). Students take turns testing each other on their respective spelling words. Collect the posttest sheets and record the correct response percentages. Mastery is 10 out of 12 words correct, or 80%. For students who do not achieve posttest mastery, see page xv in this Teacher's Edition.

After the posttest, have students select one or two anchor words to help them remember the word feature in this lesson. Record the words on the "Anchor Words" poster and refer to them in the Review lesson.

Lesson 24 Doubled Consonants (at syllable juncture). Words are divided into syllables between double consonants: for example, *swim•ming* and *ap•pear*.

Day 1
Pretest and Word Lists

Day 1 Word Lists — In the Pretest column, write the words your teacher says. When your list is ready for the week, copy it in the School and At-Home Lists.

Pretest

1._____
2._____
3._____
4._____
5._____
6._____
7._____
8._____
9._____
10._____
11._____
12._____

School List

1._____
2._____
3._____
4._____
5._____
6._____
7._____
8._____
9._____
10._____
11._____
12._____

Lesson 24 At-Home List

name _____

1._____
2._____
3._____
4._____
5._____
6._____
7._____
8._____
9._____
10._____
11._____
12._____

Before Photocopy the Answer Key/Shopping List page (page 116 in this Teacher's Edition) for each student.

During Say each word in bold, read the context sentence, and repeat the word. Have students record the pretest words in the pretest column on page 93 of the Student Book.

After Distribute to students a copy of the Answer Key/Shopping List page so that they can correct their pretests.

- Students should cross out any misspelled words and write the correct spelling. Words that were correctly spelled can be replaced with words from the Shopping List. Identify the list from which students should choose their words. (See below.)

- Be sure that each student has a list of twelve correctly spelled words, which they should copy into the School and At-Home Lists and the Sorting Boxes (page 116).

Pretest context sentences (spelling word in bold)

1. Let's go **swimming** in the pool.
2. The sun will **appear** when that cloud moves away.
3. The surprise **happened** when Shelly least expected it.
4. When things are not the same, they are **different**.
5. Mom **allowed** me to go outside after I finished my homework.
6. The lottery grand prize is one **million** dollars.
7. The carpenter used his **hammer** and nails to build my closet.
8. Kevin was so **unhappy** that he began to cry.
9. If I fail the test, I would really **disappoint** my parents.
10. The **squirrel** raced up the tree with an acorn in its mouth.
11. Whales have large amounts of **blubber**.
12. John's hands were **clammy** because he was very nervous.

At-Home List Send the At-Home List home so that families can use the following activities with their students: doubled consonants, alternate spelling.

NOTE The Shopping List provides words below grade level (the first two rows), at grade level (the middle two rows), and above grade level (the last two rows).

Name _____

Answer Key

1. swimming   7. hammer
2. appear   8. unhappy
3. happened   9. disappoint
4. different   10. squirrel
5. allowed   11. blubber
6. million   12. clammy

Shopping List

| planning | common | cannot | giggle |
| apply | setting | dollar | dazzling |

| meddle | brittle | tunnels | opportunities |
| wriggled | cobblestone | scuffled | accomplishments |

| straggled | professor | grapple | scrimmage |
| smitten | pollution | whittle | summertime |

Sorting Boxes

Day 2
Word Sorting

Encourage students to read their word lists and think about the words, looking for generalizations that they can make about how the words are similar or different. Have students sort the words, which shows you what they understand about them. The written generalization is evidence of their thought process.

- If students have not figured out what the words have in common, model for students a way to sort, using all the words. Be certain to elicit ideas from the students that draw them to the common conclusion. You can use oversized word cards (CD-ROM) or a cut-up transparency (Transparency 22) and overhead to facilitate your model.

- Guide students to discover that when part of a word follows the VCCV pattern, it should be divided into syllables between the doubled consonant. Review the meaning of VCCV (Vowel Consonant Consonant Vowel), as needed.

- Guide students to sort by looking for the doubled consonant letter in each word. Then ask several volunteers how they would break the VCCV part of the word into syllables (at the doubled consonant). Note that the vowel that precedes the doubled consonant never has a long sound. This is why consonants in short vowel words are doubled before the ending, to preserve the vowel sound (*swimming*).

- Caution students to be aware of the consonants across the syllable breaks when they write words of two or more syllables. A common spelling error is to include only one consonant where there should be two: for example, *hamer* for *hammer*.

- Help students verbalize the generalization: *When part of a word contains the VCCV pattern, break the syllables between the doubled consonant.*

- Have students write the generalization in their Student Book (page 94). You might also write the generalization on a sentence strip or poster to display for the duration of the lesson. Leave room for students to add some of their Prove It! words from Day 3.

- Have students store their Sorting Boxes. (See page xi in this Teacher's Edition.)

Students should review the generalization from Day 2: *When part of a word contains the VCCV pattern, break the syllables between the doubled consonant.* Then send them off to find in readable materials more examples that prove the generalization to be true. Tell students that they must be able to read and pronounce any word they find and record for the activity. Adjust the amount and kind of reading material students will use and the number of words they should find, according to their needs. Keep the Prove It! lists to put in a class word bank or chart for future reference.

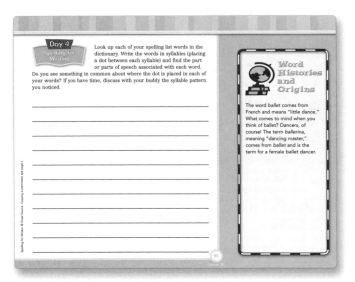

Have students look up all their spelling list words in the dictionary, write each word in syllables (by placing a dot between syllables), and write the part/parts of speech for each word.

Remind students to

- double-check what they have copied from the dictionary.

- be certain they have included all the parts of speech relevant to the word notice the pattern of syllabication of their words.

Proofreading Tip Every student should be able to copy words accurately if they are careful. Suggest that students touch each letter in the word they copied to compare it with the original source. If students are working together, one child can spell the copied word aloud while the other follows along in the original source.

WORD HISTORY Students may be curious to know the origin of the name of another popular dance form—the Twist. The word *twist* comes from the Germanic base *twi-*, meaning "doubled." In Old English, *twi-* was found in compound words referring to items made with pairs (or doubles) of things, such as ropes formed from two strands. (It is also present in <u>twi</u>ce and <u>twi</u>ns.) In the fourteenth century, *twist* appeared as an independent word associated with "wrench"—a verb meaning "to twist" or a noun meaning "a tool for turning."

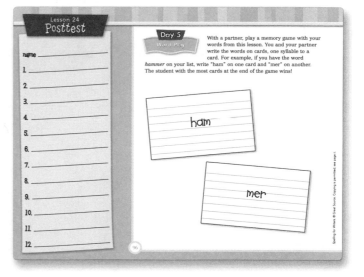

Have student partners play a memory game with their words. Have students find a partner and write their words on cards, separating the words into syllables. Each student writes his or her words on cards—one syllable to a card. For example, a student with the word *hammer* writes "ham" on one card and "mer" on another. Students take turns flipping over two cards to see if they match to form a spelling word. If the cards do not match, the student flips the cards back over and puts them in the same position. Then it's the partner's turn. If the cards do match up and form a spelling word, the student takes possession of the two cards. The student with the most cards at the end wins.

Keep the cards in a word study center or other accessible place for students to use in their spare time to reinforce the word feature.

Posttest Have students tear out the perforated posttest. Students should pair up with their buddies or partners and exchange School Lists (page 93 in the Student Book). Students take turns testing each other on their respective spelling words. Collect the posttest sheets and record the correct response percentages. Mastery is 10 out of 12 words correct, or 80%. For students who do not achieve posttest mastery, see page xv in this Teacher's Edition.

After the posttest, have students select one or two anchor words to help them remember the word feature in this lesson. Record the words on the "Anchor Words" poster and refer to them in the Review lesson.

Periodically, check writing samples from your students for transfer of the features that have been taught. The features for the last three lessons follow:

Lesson 22: Preconsonant Nasals
Lesson 23: Vowel Alternations
Lesson 24: Doubled Consonants (at syllable juncture)

Lesson 25 — R-controlled Vowels.

When a vowel is followed by *r*, the *r* influences (or controls) the sound of the vowel, as in *scar* and *author*.

Before Photocopy the Answer Key/ Shopping List page (page 121 in this Teacher's Edition) for each student.

During Say each word in bold, read the context sentence, and repeat the word. Have students record the pretest words in the pretest column on page 97 of the Student Book.

After Distribute to students a copy of the Answer Key/Shopping List page so that they can correct their pretests.

- Students should cross out any misspelled words and write the correct spelling. Words that were correctly spelled can be replaced with words from the Shopping List. Identify the list from which students should choose their words. (See below.)

- Be sure that each student has a list of twelve correctly spelled words, which they should copy into the School and At-Home Lists and the Sorting Boxes (page 121).

Pretest context sentences (spelling word in bold)

1. Another name for a rabbit is **hare**.
2. The cut on my knee left a visible **scar**.
3. The Statue of Liberty has a **torch** in her hand.
4. Dad wakes up early in the **morning** to go to work.
5. How much is the **fare** to get on the bus?
6. When it's cold, I put a warm, woolen **scarf** around my neck.
7. The tugboat towed the heavy **barge** down the river.
8. Have you ever seen an eagle **soar** through the sky?
9. I love building sandcastles on the **seashore**!
10. The unexpected fire put us in **turmoil**.
11. Look at the snake over **there**.
12. Who is the **author** of your favorite book?

At-Home List

Send the At-Home List home so that families can use the following activities with their students: word search, rhyming words.

NOTE The Shopping List provides words below grade level (the first two rows), at grade level (the middle two rows), and above grade level (the last two rows).

Name _____

Answer Key

1. hare	**7.** barge
2. scar	**8.** soar
3. torch	**9.** seashore
4. morning	**10.** turmoil
5. fare	**11.** there
6. scarf	**12.** author

Shopping List

our	where	heard	warm
different	another	parties	cork
you're	wart	unicorn	folklore
favorite	boar	hoard	square
lair	marvelous	loiter	thermal
ordeal	somersault	monarchy	literacy

Sorting Boxes

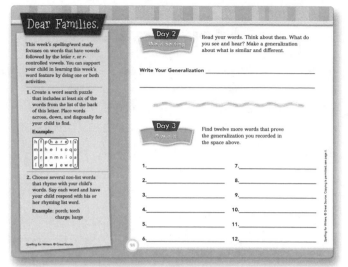

Day 2
Word Sorting

Have students look at the words carefully and decide for themselves a way or ways in which they can sort the words (do an open sort). Once they have made their sorts, have them write a generalization about the words. How students think about the words shows you what they understand about them. The written generalization is evidence of their thought process.

- After students do an open sort, bring the class together to come to a consensus. If students have not or cannot come to consensus, model for them a way to sort using all the words. You can use oversized word cards (CD-ROM) or a cut-up transparency (Transparency 23) and overhead to facilitate your model.

- Guide students to discover that when *r* follows one or more vowels, the *r* influences (or controls) the sound of the vowel(s).

- Select words at random. Have students pronounce them with you as they look at each word. Ask volunteers to identify the vowel letter or letters influenced by *r*. For example, say the word *soaring*. Students should identify *oa* as the vowel pair influenced by *r*. Compare the sound of *oa* in *soaring* and *moat* to make the difference clear to students.

- Help students state a generalization based on the activity: *When* r *follows one or more vowels, the* r *controls the vowel sound.*

- Have students write a generalization to describe the words in their Student Book (page 98). You might also write the generalization on a sentence strip or poster to display for the duration of the lesson. Leave room for students to add some of their Prove It! words from Day 3.

- Have students store their Sorting Boxes. (See page xi in this Teacher's Edition.)

Day 3

Prove It!

Students should review the generalization from Day 2: *When* r *follows one or more vowels, the* r *influences (or controls) the sound of the vowel(s).* Then send them off to find in readable materials more examples that prove the generalization to be true. Tell students that they must be able to read and pronounce any word they find and record for the activity. Adjust the amount and kind of reading material students will use and the number of words they should find, according to their needs. Keep the Prove It! lists to put in a class word bank or chart for future reference.

Day 4

Spelling for Writing

The goal of any spelling program is for students to be able to use their words in writing. Have students use as many spelling list words as they can to write clues for the words in the crossword puzzle on Student Book page 99.

Share these tips with students:

- Clues should be short but give enough information.

- Clues should be checked for correct spelling.

Proofreading Tip Because the clues have few words, it is important that they make sense and that they are complete. Suggest that students use the proofreading strategy of reading aloud to check their crossword puzzle clues. Students can whisper the words aloud so as not to disturb their neighbors.

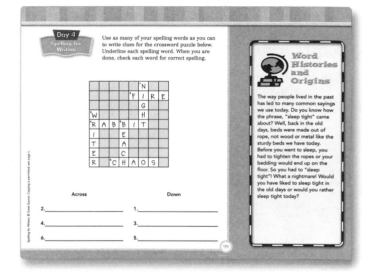

WORD HISTORY Students may be curious to know how life in the past led to the common phrase, "under the weather." Ask students what "under the weather" means (a person is not feeling well). Explain that people began saying this phrase in the 1700s. During that period, many people traveled by boat and when stormy weather came, a lot of passengers went under the deck to their cabins because they were feeling sick. Soon, saying that a person was under the deck and suffering from the influence of bad weather got shortened to "*under the weather.*" Ask students if they can recall a time when they were "under the weather."

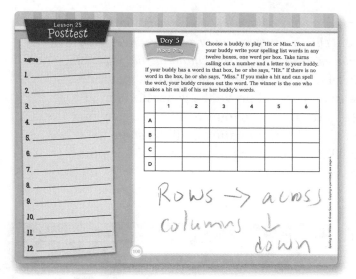

name _____
1. _____
2. _____
3. _____
4. _____
5. _____
6. _____
7. _____
8. _____
9. _____
10. _____
11. _____
12. _____

Day 5
Word Play

Choose a buddy to play "Hit or Miss." You and your buddy write your spelling list words in any twelve boxes, one word per box. Take turns calling out a number and a letter to your buddy. If your buddy has a word in that box, he or she says, "Hit." If there is no word in the box, he or she says, "Miss." If you make a hit and can spell the word, your buddy crosses out the word. The winner is the one who makes a hit on all of his or her buddy's words.

	1	2	3	4	5	6
A						
B						
C						
D						

Rows → across
columns ↓
down

Day 5
Word Play and Posttest

Have students find a partner and play "Hit or Miss." Each student should write his or her spelling list words randomly in any twelve of the twenty-four boxes of the grid, one word per box. Have partners alternate calling out a number (from one to four) and a letter (from A to F) to identify a box in their partner's grid. If a partner has a word in that box, he or she says, "Hit." If there is no word in the box, he or she says, "Miss." If one of the partners makes a hit, the other partner crosses out the word only if the player can spell the word. The winner is the partner who makes a hit on all of the other partner's words.

Posttest Have students tear out the perforated posttest. Students should pair up with their buddies or partners and exchange School Lists (page 97 in Student Book). Students take turns testing each other on their respective spelling words. Collect the posttest sheets and record the correct response percentages. Mastery is 10 out of 12 words correct, or 80%. For students who do not achieve posttest mastery, see page xv in this Teacher's Edition.

After the posttest, have students select one or two anchor words to help them remember the word feature in this lesson. Record the words on the "Anchor Words" poster and refer to them in the Review lesson.

Lesson 26

Prefixes (same base word or root). A prefix changes the meaning of a base word or root, as shown by these word pairs that have the same base or root but a different prefix (*deflate, inflate*).

Day 1
Pretest and Word Lists

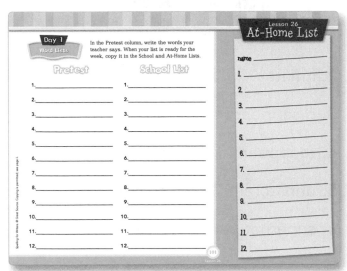

Before Photocopy the Answer Key/ Shopping List page (page 126 in this Teacher's Edition) for each student.

During Say each word in bold, read the context sentence, and repeat the word. Have students record the pretest words in the pretest column on page 101 of the Student Book.

After Distribute to students a copy of the Answer Key/Shopping List page so that they can correct their pretests.

- Students should cross out any misspelled words and write the correct spelling. Consider a pair wrong if one word was misspelled. Word pairs that were correctly spelled can be replaced with word pairs from the Shopping List. (See note below.)

- Be sure that each student has a list of six word pairs, which they should copy into the School and At-Home Lists and the Sorting Boxes (page 126).

Pretest context sentences (spelling word in bold)

1. Sticking a balloon with a pin will cause it to **deflate**.
2. I need to **inflate** all these balloons for the party.
3. The magician can make the bunny **disappear**.
4. Can the magician make the bunny **reappear**?
5. It is **unnatural** to have snowstorms in June.
6. Superheroes have many **supernatural** powers.
7. Amy is so sweet that she could **befriend** anyone.
8. The angry security guard is very **unfriendly**.
9. "Sad" is an **antonym** of "happy."
10. "Glad" is an **synonym** for "happy."
11. Decorators give much **forethought** to their design plans.
12. The decorator's last-minute decision to change the rugs was an **afterthought**.

At-Home List Send the At-Home List home so that families can use the following activities with their students: word hunt, oral spelling.

NOTE The Shopping List provides words below grade level (the first two rows), at grade level (the middle two rows), and above grade level (the last two rows).

Name _____

Answer Key

1. deflate
2. inflate
3. disappear
4. reappear
5. unnatural
6. supernatural
7. befriend
8. unfriendly
9. antonym
10. synonym
11. forethought
12. afterthought

Shopping List

induct	import	exceed	underpriced
deduct	export	proceed	overpriced
inward	disorganize	revise	proslavery
onward	reorganize	devise	antislavery
introvert	hyperactive	repair	autocracy
extrovert	hypoactive	disrepair	democracy

Sorting Boxes

Day 2
Word Sorting

Have students look at the words carefully and decide for themselves a way or ways in which they can sort the words (do an open sort). Once they have made their sorts, have them write a generalization about the words. How students think about the words shows you what they understand about them. The written generalization is evidence of their thought process.

Dear Families,

This week's spelling/word study focuses on pairs of words that have the same base or root but different prefixes, which change the meaning of the words (*inflate/ deflate, unnatural/ supernatural*). You can help your child learn the word feature by reviewing the words on the back of this letter and by doing one or both of these activities:

1. During leisure time reading, have your child look for occurrences of words on his or her list. Suggest your child keep a tally chart of the words.

2. Challenge your child with oral spelling math problems. Have him or her spell each solution.

Example: *deflate* minus *de-* plus *in-* is (*inflate*).

Spelling for Writers © Great Source.

Day 2
Word Sorting

Read your words. Think about them. What jumps out at you about these words? Write a generalization about how the words are similar or different.

Write Your Generalization _____

_____

Day 3
Prove It!

Find six more pairs of words that prove the generalization you recorded in the space above.

1._____ _____
2._____ _____
3._____ _____
4._____ _____
5._____ _____
6._____ _____

102

- After students do an open sort, bring the class together to come to a consensus. If students have not or cannot come to consensus, model for them a way to sort using all the words. You can use oversized word cards (CD-ROM) or a cut-up transparency (Transparency 24) and overhead to facilitate your model.

- Guide students to discover that a prefix changes the meaning of a base word (such as *appear*) or root (such as *flate*), which is made clear in these word pairs in which the base word or root is the same.

- Focus on how the word pairs are related in meaning, as dictated by the common base word or root. Some of the word pairs are opposites, for example, *inflate* means "to force air or gas <u>into</u> an object" and *deflate* means "to let air or gas <u>out of</u> an object."

- Suggest that students sort their words by whether the prefix is attached to a base word or a root.

- Help students state a generalization based on the activity: *A prefix changes the meaning of a base word or root.*

- Point out that no spelling change is required when the prefix is added to the base word or root.

- Have students write the generalization in their Student Book (page 102). You might also write the generalization on a sentence strip or poster to display for the duration of the lesson. Leave room for students to add some of their Prove It! words from Day 3.

- Have students store their Sorting Boxes. (See page xi in this Teacher's Edition.)

Students should review the generalization: *A prefix can change the meaning of a base word or root.* Then send them off to find in readable materials more examples that prove the generalization to be true. Tell students that they must be able to read and pronounce any word they find and record for the activity. Adjust the amount and kind of reading material students will use and the number of words they should find, according to their needs. Keep the Prove It! lists to put in a class word bank or chart for future reference.

NOTE Students may find only one word of a pair in text, such as *increase*. They can then supply a paired word, such as *decrease*.

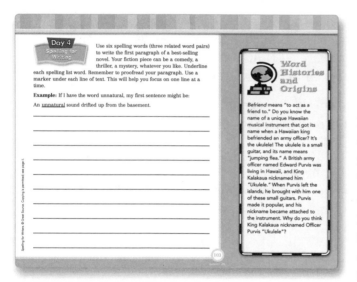

Have students use six spelling list words (three related word pairs) to write the first paragraph of a best-selling novel. Tell students that their novels can be on any topic they choose. Review the example on Student Book page 103. Before students begin to write, talk with them about how the first page of a novel has to grab the reader. It might also set the scene or introduce a character. Help students decide on the purpose of their first page so that they will have a focus for their writing. Read several first pages from age-appropriate chapter books to inspire students.

Share these tips with students:

- Work from imagination or personal experience.

- Grab readers' attention with the first sentence or two.

- Use exact words (example: *shack* instead of *house*).

- Create a picture in the reader's mind.

Proofreading Tip Remind students that accurate text is a courtesy to the reader. In other words, the reader will have an easier time getting the meaning out of a piece of writing if he or she is not distracted by mistakes. Suggest that students put a marker under each line of text as they proofread so that their eyes focus on one line at a time.

WORD HISTORY A person who appears unfriendly can be said to have "a chip on his (or her) shoulder." Tell students that this common phrase indicates that a person is quarrelsome, angry, or unfriendly. This idiom came from the early 1800s when American boys played a game in which one boy would put a wood chip on his shoulder and dare another boy to knock it off. If he did knock it off, the two boys would fight.

Day 5

Word Play and Posttest

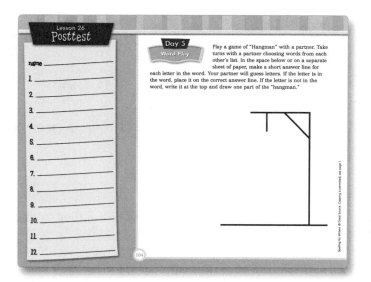

Have students play a game of "Hangman" with a partner. Partners will work from each other's lists. If students have never played "Hangman" before, play a round with the whole class. On the board, draw the hangman's frame and a short answer line for each letter in the word. When students guess a letter that is in the word, place it on the correct answer line. If the letter is not in the word, write it at the top and draw one part of the body. Decide ahead of time how many parts the body will have (i.e., how many guesses students will get).

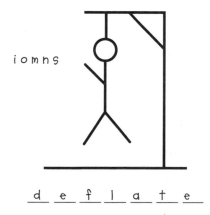

i o m n s

d e f l a t e

Posttest Have students tear out the perforated posttest. Students should pair up with their buddies or partners and exchange School Lists (page 101 in Student Book). Students take turns testing each other on their respective spelling words. Collect the posttest sheets and record the correct response percentages. Mastery is 10 out of 12 words correct, or 80%. For students who do not achieve posttest mastery, see page xv in this Teacher's Edition. After the posttest, have students select one or two anchor words to help them remember the word feature in this lesson. Record the words on the "Anchor Words" poster and refer to them in the Review lesson.

Lesson 27 Review (Lessons 21-26).

Before There are three options for selecting the pretest words. Choose the one most appropriate for your students.

1. Have students think of two words that fit the spelling pattern and write them.

2. Use the words that you and your class collected on the "Anchor Words" poster.

3. Use the examples given below.

If you will dictate the words, either from the "Anchor Words" poster or from below, write them on a copy of the Answer Key page (Teacher's Edition page 131). Photocopy the filled-in Answer Key page for each student.

During Announce each word feature. Then state the spelling generalization and give the words or tell students to think of two words. Students will write two pretest words for each feature on page 105 of the Student Book.

After If you dictated the words, distribute a copy of the Answer Key so that students can self-correct their pretests. Otherwise, correct students' pretests.

• For any word feature that students got correct, send them back to the lesson for that feature to select a word from their Prove It! list they want to learn to spell.

• Be sure that each student has a list of correctly spelled words, which they should copy into the School and At-Home Lists and the Sorting Boxes.

Word Features and Generalizations

1. **Complex Vowel Patterns.** Two side-by-side vowels can represent a vowel sound that is neither long nor short, as in *applaud*, and *fought*. (*Lesson 21*)

2. **Preconsonant Nasals.** When *m* and *n* come before another consonant letter, their nasal sounds are hard to hear, as in *champ* and *belong*. (*Lesson 22*)

3. **Vowel Alternations.** When endings are added to some words, the vowel sound can change, but the vowel letter stays the same, as in the word pairs *central/centrality* and *wide/width*. (*Lesson 23*)

(*continued on page 132*)

Name _____

Answer Key

1. applaud _____ (Lesson 21)
2. fought _____ (Lesson 21)
3. champ _____ (Lesson 22)
4. belong _____ (Lesson 22)
5. wide _____ (Lesson 23)
6. width _____ (Lesson 23)
7. different _____ (Lesson 24)
8. hammer _____ (Lesson 24)
9. turmoil _____ (Lesson 25)
10. author _____ (Lesson 25)
11. disappear _____ (Lesson 26)
12. reappear _____ (Lesson 26)

Sorting Boxes

4. **Doubled Consonants (at syllable juncture).** When part of a word follows the VCCV pattern, it should be divided into syllables between the doubled consonant, as in *different* and *hammer*. (*Lesson 24*)

5. *R*-**Controlled Vowels.** When *r* follows a vowel, the *r* influences, or controls, the vowel sound, as in *turmoil* and *author*. (*Lesson 25*)

6. **Prefixes (same base word or root).** A different prefix can change the meaning of the same base word or root, as in the word pairs *deflate/inflate* and *disappear/reappear*. (*Lesson 26*)

At-Home List Send the At-Home List home so that families can use the following activities with their children: word sorting, word hunt, word-guessing game.

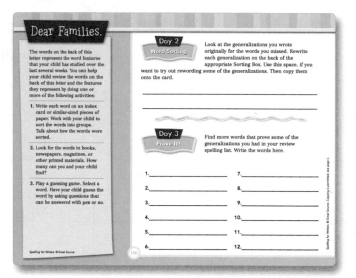

Students work with partners to revisit the generalizations for words they misspelled on the Pretest. Suggest that they look back at the generalizations they wrote in their book at time of initial study of the lesson's words. Tell them to try to reword the generalizations to help them better remember them. Even students who got all the words correct can revisit and reword several generalizations that were unclear the first time.

The rewording process should provide students insight into what "rules" govern many different sets of words. Students should rewrite their revised generalizations on the backs of their Sorting Boxes.

As a closing step, have students work in pairs to sort their words into groups that make sense. Circulate through the room to talk with students about their word sorts. The explanations of the sorts tell you what students understand about words.

After students revisit and revise the several generalizations for this week's review, send them off to find in readable materials more examples that prove as many of the generalizations as possible. Tell students that they must be able to read and

pronounce any word they find and record for the activity. Adjust the amount and kind of reading material students will use and the number of words they should find, according to their needs. Keep the Prove It! lists to put in a class word bank or chart for future reference.

Day 4
Spelling for Writing

Tell students to look at their list of spelling words and use as many of them as possible to write a story. Students can also include words from the word hunt (Prove It!). Sentences should be constructed carefully so that words are explained in context.

Tell students that

- the words they choose will help determine the content of their stories.

- all stories have a beginning, a middle, and an ending.

- dialogue helps the reader know what the characters are like and adds interest to the story.

- the sentences that contain spelling words must clearly convey the meaning of each spelling word used.

Proofreading Tip Remind students once again that reading and proofreading are different. Ask students to share which proofreading strategies they use and which ones are most helpful. Some of the strategies they might mention are the following: read for one item at a time, touch each word with a pencil point, read the words aloud, look for errors the writer commonly makes, and work with a partner.

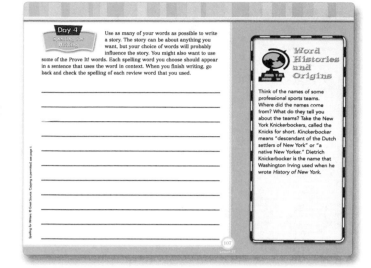

Word Histories and Origins Students are told about the origin of name of the New York basketball team, the Knickerbockers. Encourage students to find out the origin of the names of other professional sports teams. For example, the Los Angeles Lakers used to play in Minnesota, the land of ten thousand lakes.

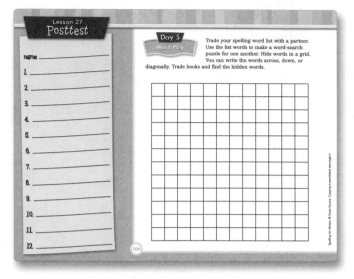

Have students swap spelling lists and create a word find for each other. Words should be hidden in a grid and can be placed so they can be read horizontally, vertically, or diagonally. Once the words are in place, students should fill the grid with random letters that do not form words. Once the word searches are ready, have the partners trade books and find the hidden words.

Other activities that students can do to review the words include the following:

- Have students choose a set of Sorting Boxes from a previous week and time themselves when they sort the cards. Students should sort the cards several times to improve their sorting time. (Copy Masters of the pretest words can be found in the Transparencies and Copy Masters folder. Or, generate word cards from the CD-ROM.)

- Students can use their review list to play one of the Word Play games from a previous lesson: for example, "Hangman," "Hit or Miss," or "Bull's Eye." They could also make a crossword puzzle.

- Generate a practice activity from the CD-ROM.

Posttest   Have students carefully tear out the posttest form on the Student Book page 76. Students should pair up with their buddies or partners and exchange School Lists (page 74 in the Student Book). Students take turns testing each other on their respective spelling words. Mastery is 80% of the number of words they had for the week (10 correct out of 12). For students who do not achieve posttest mastery, see page xi in this Teacher's Edition.

Lesson 28 Prefixes and Suffixes. Prefixes and suffixes change the meaning of a word.
Sometimes a word has both a prefix and a suffix (*disabled, unwinding*).

Day 1
Pretest and Word Lists

Before Photocopy the Answer Key/ Shopping List page (page 136 in this Teacher's Edition) for each student.

During Say each word in bold, read the context sentence, and repeat the word. Have students record the pretest words in the pretest column on page 109 of the Student Book.

After Distribute to students a copy of the Answer Key/Shopping List page so that they can correct their pretests.

- Students should cross out any misspelled words and write the correct spelling. Words that were correctly spelled can be replaced with words from the Shopping List. Identify the list from which students should choose their words. (See below.)

- Be sure that each student has a list of twelve correctly spelled words, which they should copy into the School and At-Home Lists and the Sorting Boxes (page 136).

Pretest context sentences (spelling word in bold)

1. She is **fulfilling** her dream of becoming a doctor by going to medical school.
2. The police officer **disabled** the bomb so that it wouldn't explode.
3. The string on my kite was **unwinding** too fast!
4. The **unhappiest** child was crying.
5. Mountains are **immovable** features in the natural world.
6. Jenna's paper had an **uncorrected** mistake on it.
7. Bill **repacked** his luggage four times to get everything to fit.
8. The old piece of tape was **unstickable**.
9. The boring reunion was **uneventful**.
10. The special effects in the movie were **unbelievable**!
11. The minor league team has been **underrated**.
12. **Semiskilled** laborers may have a hard time finding jobs that pay well.

At-Home List Send the At-Home List home so that families can use the following activities with their students: speed spelling, sum of the parts.

NOTE The Shopping List provides words below grade level (the first four rows), at grade level (the middle four rows), and above grade level (the last four rows).

Name _____

Answer Key

1. fulfilling
2. disabled
3. unwinding
4. unhappiest
5. immovable
6. uncorrected
7. repacked
8. unstickable
9. uneventful
10. unbelievable
11. underrated
12. semiskilled

Shopping List

compressed	replanted
redirection	uneasily
untouchable	undersized
reaction	recreation
unoriginal	unlatched
transferred	transplanted
imperfection	investment
semiclosed	declared
inflatable	unemployed
forewarned	commitment
derailed	antibacterial
descendant	illogical

Sorting Boxes

Day 2
Word Sorting

Have students look at the words carefully and decide for themselves a way or ways in which they can sort the words (do an open sort). Once they have made their sorts, have them write a generalization about the words. How students think about the words shows you what they under-stand about them. The written generaliza-tion is evidence of their thought process.

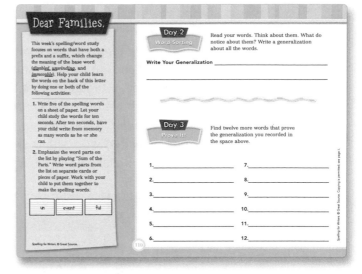

- After students do an open sort, bring the class together to come to a consensus. If students have not or cannot come to consensus, model for them a way to sort using all the words. You can use oversized word cards (CD-ROM) or a cut-up transparen-cy (Transparency 25) and overhead to facilitate your model.

- Guide them to discover that when a prefix or suffix is added to a word, it changes the meaning of the base word and that words can have both a prefix and a suffix.

- First, help students identify the base word for each word. Then have students sort the words by their different prefixes. Then have students sort according to the different suffixes.

- After students successfully make their prefix and suffix sorts, talk briefly about the meanings of the different prefixes and suffixes and how they change the word.

  -ful (full of) *dis-*, *un-*, *im-* (not)

  re- (again) *semi-* (half or partial)

- Remind students that prefixes rarely cause a spelling change in a base word or root. However, the addition of a suffix (or inflection) often results in a spelling change. Ask students to identify words whose base word or root underwent a spelling change when the suffix was added. Examples include *disabled* (drop *e*), *unhappiest* (change *y* to *i*), and *transferred* (double consonant).

- Model for students how to make a statement about how all their words were sorted: *Some words can have both a prefix and a suffix, each of which changes the mean-ing of the word.*

- Have students write the generalization in their Student Book (page 110). You might also write the generalization on a sentence strip or poster to display for the dura-tion of the lesson. Leave room for students to add some of their Prove It! words from Day 3.

- Have students store their Sorting Boxes. (See page xi in this Teacher's Edition.)

Students should review the generalization from Day 2: *When a prefix or suffix is added to a word, it changes the meaning of the base word.* Then send them off to find in readable materials more examples that prove the generalization to be true. Tell students that they must be able to read and pronounce any word they find and record for the activity. Adjust the amount and kind of reading material students will use and the number of words they should find, according to their needs. Keep the Prove It! lists to put in a class word bank or chart for future reference.

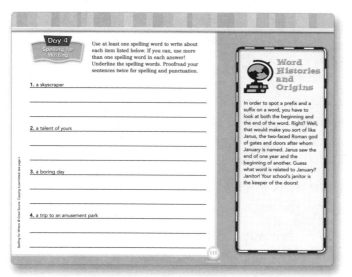

Students will use at least one spelling word to write about each item on Student Book page 111. Challenge students to stretch their thinking and use more than one spelling word in their responses! Sample answers:

1. A skyscraper is an <u>immovable</u> object.
2. I know how to stack cards to make a house, a talent that is quite <u>underrated</u>.
3. Yesterday was completely <u>uneventful</u>. Nothing happened all day.
4. I <u>repacked</u> my backpack four times before I left for the amusement park.

Proofreading Tip A key to careful proofreading is to check for one item at a time. Tell students to proofread their sentences twice, once for sentence form (capital letter at the beginning, punctuation at the end) and once for spelling.

WORD HISTORY Students may be curious to know the origin of another month name, *March.* Tell students that before Julius Caesar changed the calendar months (explained in Lesson 11), the Roman New Year began with the month of March. This month was also the opening spring season for waging wars, so the month was dedicated to Mars, the god of war, and was named after him.

Day 5
Word Play and Posttest

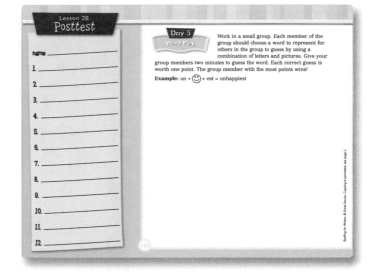

Students are to convey a word to their classmates through drawings and letters. Students can play the game in a small group (as described on Student Book page 112) or the whole class can play in teams. For the whole class to play, put all the word cards for this lesson (CD-ROM) in a hat. Group the students into several small teams. A student from each team picks a word card from the hat and uses a combination of letters and sketches to represent the word to his or her teammates. The team has two minutes to guess the correct word. Each correct guess is worth one point. The team with the most points after all the words have been chosen wins the game.

Posttest Have students tear out the perforated posttest. Students should pair up with their buddies or partners and exchange School Lists (page 109 in the Student Book). Students take turns testing each other on their respective spelling words. Collect the posttest sheets and record the correct response percentages. Mastery is 10 out of 12 words correct, or 80%. For students who do not achieve posttest mastery, see page xv in this Teacher's Edition.

After the posttest, have students select one or two anchor words to help them remember the word feature in this lesson. Record the words on the "Anchor Words" poster and refer to them in the Review lesson.

Periodically, check writing samples from your students for transfer of the word features that have been taught. The features for the last three lessons are as follows:

Lesson 25: R-controlled Vowels
Lesson 26: Prefixes (same base word or root)
Lesson 28: Prefixes and Suffixes

Lesson 29 Doubled Consonants (at syllable juncture). When a word follows the VCCV pattern, syllables are divided between the two consonants, as in flam•mable.

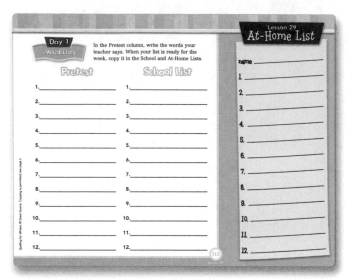

Day 1
Pretest and Word Lists

Before Photocopy the Answer Key/ Shopping List page (page 141 in this Teacher's Edition) for each student.

During Say each word in bold, read the context sentence, and repeat the word. Have students record the pretest words in the pretest column on page 113 of the Student Book.

After Distribute to students a copy of the Answer Key/Shopping List page so that they can correct their pretests.

- Students should cross out any misspelled words and write the correct spelling. Words that were correctly spelled can be replaced with words from the Shopping List. Identify the list from which students should choose their words. (See below.)

- Be sure that each student has a list of twelve correctly spelled words, which they should copy into the School and At-Home Lists and the Sorting Boxes (page 141).

Pretest context sentences (spelling word in bold)

1. Hairspray is extremely **flammable,** so keep it away from high heat.
2. Homeowners **grapple** with the problem of basement flooding.
3. I can make bacon and eggs on the **griddle**.
4. The stars were **glittering** in the night sky.
5. The police think the criminal will **surrender**.
6. Do you have the **current** issue of this magazine?
7. The mole will **burrow** a hole for shelter.
8. The **hurricane** winds reached 112 miles per hour.
9. Crossing streets at the crosswalk is **allowable**.
10. The **cunning** fox steals our chickens all the time.
11. Itchy hives are a common symptom of **allergy**.
12. Sue **chopped** wood for the fireplace.

At-Home List Send the At-Home List home so that families can use the following activities with their students: fill in sentences, category words for letters.

NOTE The Shopping List provides words below grade level (the first four rows), at grade level (the middle four rows), and above grade level (the last four rows).

Name _____

Answer Key

1. flammable
2. grapple
3. griddle
4. glittering
5. surrender
6. current
7. burrow
8. hurricane
9. allowable
10. cunning
11. allergy
12. chopped

Shopping List

grinning	stopped
patted	tapping
rubbed	settle
wrapped	supper
merriment	blizzard
summit	channels
appearance	saddened
suddenly	gallons
commute	assertive
transferred	recommendation
communities	immediately
sufficient	cancellation

Sorting Boxes

Lesson 29

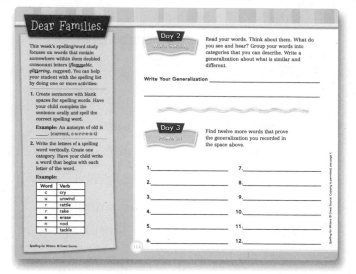

Have students look at the words carefully and decide for themselves a way or ways in which they can sort the words (do an open sort). Once they have made their sorts, have them write a generalization about the words. How students think about the words shows you what they understand about them. The written generalization is evidence of their thought process.

- After students do an open sort, bring the class together to come to a consensus. If students have not or cannot come to consensus, model for them a way to sort using all the words. You can use oversized word cards (CD-ROM) or a cut-up transparency (Transparency 26) and overhead to facilitate your model.

- Guide students to discover that when part of a word follows the VCCV (vowel-consonant-consonant-vowel) pattern, it should be divided into syllables between the doubled consonant.

- Call attention to several words, one at a time. Have students identify the part of the word that has a VCCV pattern. Ask them to name the doubled letter.

- Have students say how they would break that portion of the word into syllables.

- Help students state the generalization: *When part of a word contains the VCCV pattern, it should be divided into syllables between the doubled consonant.*

- Understanding this generalization will help students break words apart for pronunciation (the first vowel in the VCCV pattern almost always has a short vowel sound or the sound of schwa) and divide words at the end of a line. In addition, when students understand one syllable of a word, they can focus their attention on the rest of the word, the spelling of which may be less certain.

- Then model how to sort the words by the total number of syllables in each. Use *glittering* as an example (three syllables: glit•ter•ing).

- After students complete their sorts, have them write the generalization in their Student Book (page 114). You might also write the generalization on a sentence strip or poster to display for the duration of the lesson. Leave room for students to add some of their Prove It! words from Day 3.

- Have students store their Sorting Boxes. (See page xi in this Teacher's Edition.)

Day 3
Prove It!

Students should review the generalization from Day 2: *When part of a word contains the VCCV pattern, the syllable break is between the doubled consonant.* Then send them off to find in readable materials more examples that prove the generalization to be true. Tell students that they must be able to read and pronounce any word they find and record for the activity. Adjust the amount and kind of reading material students will use and the number of words they should find, according to their needs. Keep the Prove It! lists to put in a class word bank or chart for future reference.

Day 4
Spelling for Writing

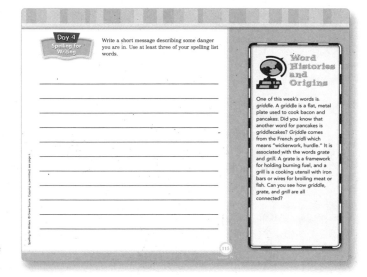

Have students use at least three of their spelling list words in a short message describing some danger they are in. Tell students that the message can describe any danger they choose.

Remind students to do the following:

- Try to convey a sense of urgency in the message.

- Reread the message for sense and correct capitalization and punctuation.

- Count the spelling list words included.

Proofreading Tip A key to careful proofreading is to look for something specific. Sometimes writers have a tendency to make errors consistently (for example, a writer might have a problem with *their, there,* and *they're*). Students should be aware of this and make a personal checklist to use when proofreading their writing.

WORD HISTORY Griddles are just the right cookware for an all-American favorite food—pancakes. Ask students what they think about when they hear the word *pancakes.* Syrup! Tell students that *syrup* comes from the Arabic *sharab,* which means "a drink." Arab drinks tend to be sweetened, so when the word was adopted into the English language it referred to a "thick, sweet liquid," just like syrup on your pancakes!

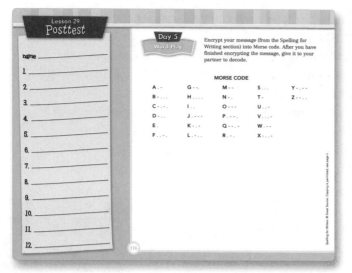

Have student encrypt their messages from the Spelling for Writing section into Morse code. After students finish encrypting the message, have students trade the message with partners. Partners should try to decode the message. Have students refer to the Morse code chart on Student Book page 116.

Posttest Have students tear out the perforated posttest. Students should pair up with their buddies or partners and exchange School Lists (page 113 in the Student Book). Students take turns testing each other on their respective spelling words. Collect the posttest sheets and record the correct response percentages. Mastery is 10 out of 12 words correct, or 80%. For students who do not achieve posttest mastery, see page xv in this Teacher's Edition.

After the posttest, have students select one or two anchor words to help them remember the word feature in this lesson. Record the words on the "Anchor Words" poster and refer to them in the Review lesson.

Lesson 30

Irregular Plurals. Plural words are formed in different ways (*knives, teeth*). Some words do not change when they are used as a plural (*deer*).

Day 1
Pretest and Word Lists

Before Photocopy the Answer Key/ Shopping List page (page 146 in this Teacher's Edition) for each student.

During Say each word in bold, read the context sentence, and repeat the word. Have students record the pretest words in the pretest column on page 117 of the Student Book.

After Distribute to students a copy of the Answer Key/Shopping List page so that they can correct their pretests.

- Students should cross out any misspelled words and write the correct spelling. Words that were correctly spelled can be replaced with words from the Shopping List. Identify the list from which students should choose their words. (See below.)

- Be sure that each student has a list of twelve correctly spelled words, which they should copy into the School and At-Home Lists and the Sorting Boxes (page 146).

Pretest context sentences (spelling word in bold)

1. We have our kitchen **knives** sharpened at the hardware store.
2. **Deer** come into our yard and eat plants and shrubs.
3. Ten **children** attend this nursery school.
4. The baseball players **wives** collected food for charity.
5. The **men** at the barbeque started to grill the burgers.
6. The dentist will check my **teeth**.
7. Three singers have **solos** in this performance.
8. My uncle and grandfather were both **firemen**.
9. The encyclopedia collection has so much **data** in it.
10. Twelve **geese** just flew overhead in a V formation.
11. I saw two **mice** in the field.
12. There is an old fairy tale about a shoemaker and some **elves**.

At-Home List Send the At-Home List home so that families can use the following activities with their students: writing plural forms, word hunt.

NOTE The Shopping List provides words below grade level (the first two rows), at grade level (the middle two rows), and above grade level (the last two rows).

Name _____

Answer Key

1. knives
2. deer
3. children
4. wives
5. men
6. teeth
7. solos
8. firemen
9. data
10. geese
11. mice
12. elves

Shopping List

| pianos | videos | moose | thieves |
| patios | leaves | dwarves | halves |

| selves | oxen | fish | women |
| loaves | vetoes | criteria | journeys |

| cacti | series | parentheses | passersby |
| foci | indices | calves | brothers-in-law |

Sorting Boxes

Day 2

Word Sorting

Have students look at the words carefully and decide for themselves a way or ways in which they can sort the words (do an open sort). Once they have made their sorts, have them write a generalization about the words. How students think about the words shows you what they understand about them. The written generalization is evidence of their thought process.

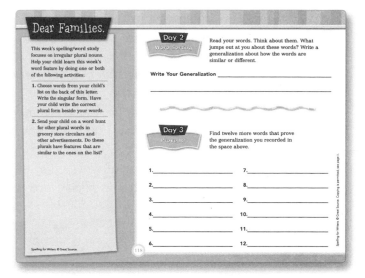

- After students do an open sort, bring the class together to come to a consensus. If students have not or cannot come to consensus, model for them a way to sort using all the words. You can use oversized word cards (CD-ROM) or a cut-up transparency (Transparency 27) and overhead to facilitate your model.

- Guide students to discover that all the words are plurals. Most of the words are irregular plurals that reflect a change in form. Some words however, simply have *-s* or *-es* at the end to signal the plural or do not change at all.

- Students' general categories for the sorting should reflect these spelling alterations: *f* to *v*, *us* to *i*, word form change, addition of *–s* or *–es*, or no spelling change at all. The number of sorting groups depends on the words on each student's list. Suggest that students identify each base word to help them recognize the spelling changes.

- Call on students to make a statement about how all their words were sorted: *All the words are plurals. They were sorted by their spelling changes:* f *to* v, us *to* i, *word form change, or no change.*

- Have students write the generalization in their Student Book (page 118). You might also write the generalization on a sentence strip or poster to display for the duration of the lesson. Leave room for students to add some of their Prove It! words from Day 3.

- Have students store their Sorting Boxes. (See page xi in this Teacher's Edition.)

Students should review the generalization from Day 2: *All the words are plurals. Most of the words are irregular plurals that reflect a change in form. Some words however, simply have s or es at the end to signal the plural.* Then send them off to find in readable materials more examples that prove the generalization to be true. Tell students that they must be able to read and pronounce any word they find and record for the activity. Adjust the amount and kind of reading material students will use and the number of words they should find, according to their needs. Keep the Prove It! lists to put in a class word bank or chart for future reference.

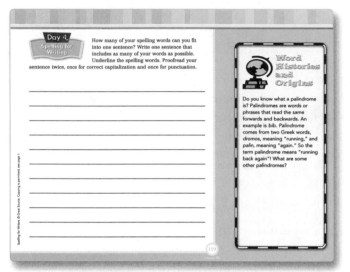

Day 4

Spelling for Writing

Students will use as many of their spelling words as they can in a single sentence. If students complete their sentences quickly, challenge them to write another sentence using a different set of words.

Proofreading Tip Remind students that reading and proofreading are different. When proofreading, students need to slow their pace so that they can examine each word. To help show them down, suggest that they touch each word with a pencil point.

WORD HISTORY Discuss other palindrome words that students may have thought about. Common responses may include *madam, mom, dad, pop, pup, level,* and *did.* Now write these three statements on the board or on chart paper. 1) Madam, I'm Adam. 2) Go hang a salami, I'm a lasagna hog! and 3) Sit on a pan, Otis! Ask students what is special about these three phrases. If students have no idea, tell them to read each phrase backwards. Students should discover that the phrases are also palindromes. If there is time, help students come up with a few palindrome phrases. Here are some examples.

Dee saw a seed   Never odd or even
Pull up if I pull up   Was it a car or a cat I saw?

Day 5

Word Play and Posttest

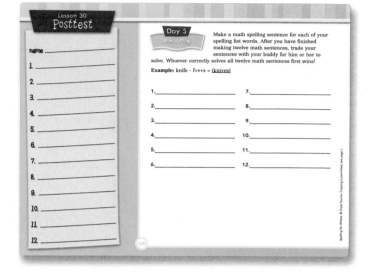

Have students make math spelling sentences for all of their spelling list words. After students make their math sentences, have them trade sentences with their partners. The partner that correctly answers all math spelling sentences first wins! Copies of students math spelling sentences could be placed in a word center or other place that is easy for students to access during spare time.

Posttest Have students tear out the perforated posttest. Students should pair up with their buddies or partners and exchange School Lists (page 117 in Student Book). Students take turns testing each other on their respective spelling words. Collect the posttest sheets and record the correct response percentages. Mastery is 10 out of 12 words correct, or 80%. For students who do not achieve posttest mastery, see page xv in this Teacher's Edition.

After the posttest, have students select one or two anchor words to help them remember the word feature in this lesson. Record the words on the "Anchor Words" poster and refer to them in the Review lesson.

Lesson 31 — Compound Words.

A compound word is made up of separate words that come together to make a new word that has its own meaning (*alongside, beehive*).

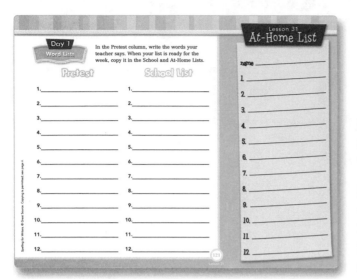

Before Photocopy the Answer Key/Shopping List page (page 151 in this Teacher's Edition) for each student.

During Say each word in bold, read the context sentence, and repeat the word. Have students record the pretest words in the pretest column on page 121 of the Student Book.

After Distribute to students a copy of the Answer Key/Shopping List page so that they can correct their pretests.

- Students should cross out any misspelled words and write the correct spelling. Words that were correctly spelled can be replaced with words from the Shopping List. Identify the list from which students should choose their words. (See below.)

- Be sure that each student has a list of twelve correctly spelled words, which they should copy into the School and At-Home Lists and the Sorting Boxes (page 151).

Pretest context sentences (spelling word in bold)

1. Notice the wildflowers growing **alongside** the river.
2. The students found fossils and a very old **arrowhead** in the cave.
3. Look at all those bees buzzing around the **beehive**!
4. The **blacksmith** made a beautiful iron sculpture.
5. The **businessmen** have an important meeting this morning.
6. We can't play checkers without the **checkerboard**!
7. My mom has to go to the **courthouse** because she has jury duty.
8. Anyone who lives in the same nation as you is your **countryman**.
9. Did you read the homework in the **textbook** last night?
10. There were mosquitoes **throughout** the entire park.
11. **Windmills** are mostly used to pump water.
12. Dad says I should spend my time on **worthwhile** reading.

At-Home List

Send the At-Home List home so that families can use the following activities with their students: new compound words, make words.

NOTE The Shopping List provides words below grade level (the first two rows), at grade level (the middle two rows), and above grade level (the last two rows).

Name _____

Answer Key

1. alongside	**7.** courthouse
2. arrowhead	**8.** countryman
3. beehive	**9.** textbook
4. blacksmith	**10.** throughout
5. businessmen	**11.** windmill
6. checkerboard	**12.** worthwhile

Shopping List

airline	bathroom	butterfly	daytime
anyway	birdbath	corncob	eyelid
inland	highlands	proofread	seaweed
lowlands	handkerchief	runaway	underground
backbone	boldface	coastline	furthermore
basketball	chairperson	coffeepot	farewell

Sorting Boxes

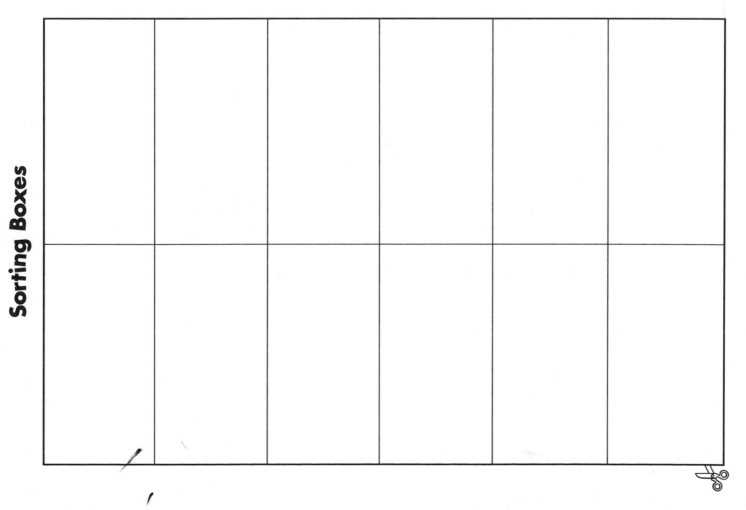

Lesson 31

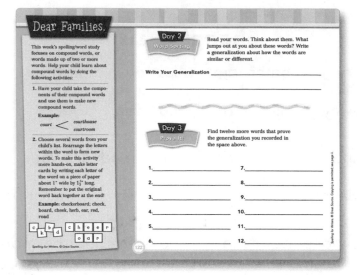

Have students look at the words carefully and decide for themselves a way or ways in which they can sort the words (do an open sort). Once they have made their sorts, have them write a generalization about the words. How students think about the words shows you what they understand about them. The written generalization is evidence of their thought process.

- After students do an open sort, bring the class together to come to a consensus. If students have not or cannot come to consensus, model for them a way to sort using all the words. You can use oversized word cards (CD-ROM) or a cut-up transparency (Transparency 28) and overhead to facilitate your model.

- Guide students to discover that all the words are compound words, or words that are formed by two words coming together to make a new word that has its own meaning.

- Generally, neither word changes its spelling when a compound word is formed. Therefore, if students can spell the two words, they can spell the compound word.

- If appropriate for your students, point out that *businessmen* is sometimes made more inclusive of women in the form *businesspeople*. Either term is correct, but the latter is often used in reference to females.

- Have students write the generalization in their Student Book (page 122). You might also write the generalization on a sentence strip or poster to display for the duration of the lesson. Leave room for students to add some of their Prove It words from Day 3.

- Have students store their Sorting Boxes. (See page xi in this Teacher's Edition.)

Day 3
Prove It!

Students should review the generalization from Day 2: *All the words are compound words, or words that are formed by two words coming together to make a new word that has its own meaning.* Then send them off to find in readable materials more examples that prove the generalization to be true. Tell students that they must be able to read and pronounce any word they find and record for the activity. Adjust the amount and kind of reading material students will use and the number of words they should find, according to their needs. To expose each student to more words, ask students to share their lists aloud with a partner or the class. Keep the Prove It! lists to put in a class word bank or chart for future reference.

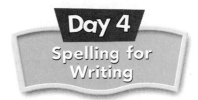

Day 4
Spelling for Writing

The goal of any spelling program is for students to be able to use their words in writing. Have students write a haiku poem that uses at least two of their spelling list words. Review the haiku poem example on Student Book page 123 with students, highlighting the poem's special features:

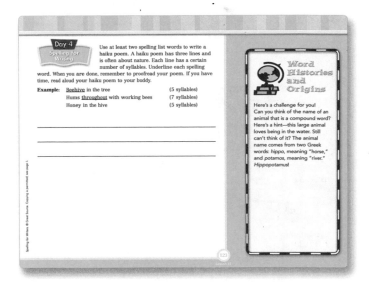

- A haiku has three lines.

- The subject is usually nature.

- The first line has five syllables, the second line has seven syllables, and the last line has five syllables.

Remind students to do the following:

- Reread the poem to see that it meets the criteria for a haiku.

- Be certain to have included at least two spelling list words and underlined them.

- Say the haiku aloud softly to try to "see" the picture.

Proofreading Tip Tell students that it is easy for a reader's eyes to skip quickly over words when there are just a few words, as in a haiku. Remind them to look at each word individually. Suggest that students touch each word with a pencil point.

WORD HISTORY Students may be curious to know about another animal name that is a compound word— *dinosaur*. Tell students that Sir Richard Owen, a British naturalist, was responsible for giving these extinct creatures their name. To him, these prehistoric monsters looked so frightful that he combined the Greek words *deinos*, meaning "fearful," with *sauros*, meaning "lizard." So, dinosaurs were lizards of which we should have been fearful!

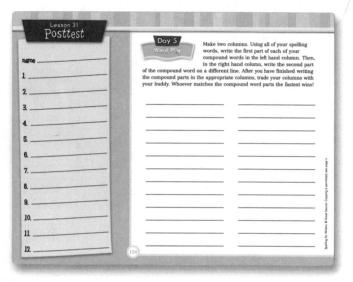

Day 5
Word Play and Posttest

In the left hand column on Student Book page 124, students should write the first part of each of their compound words. Then in the right hand column, they should write the second part of their compound words, but on a different line (so that the word parts are mixed up). After students have finished writing the compound parts in the appropriate columns, they should trade their columns with a partner. The first partner to correctly match all compound parts wins!

Posttest Have students tear out the perforated posttest. Students should pair up with their buddies or partners and exchange School Lists (page 121 in the Student Book). Students take turns testing each other on their respective spelling words. Collect the posttest sheets and record the correct response percentages. Mastery is 10 out of 12 words correct, or 80%. For students who do not achieve posttest mastery, see page xv in this Teacher's Edition.

After the posttest, have students select one or two anchor words to help them remember the word feature in this lesson. Record the words on the "Anchor Words" poster and refer to them in the Review lesson.

Periodically, check writing samples from your students for transfer of the word features that have been taught. The features for the last three lessons are as follows:

Lesson 29: Doubled Consonant (at syllable juncture)
Lesson 30: Irregular Plurals
Lesson 31: Compound Words

Lesson 32

Homonyms. Words that sound the same but are spelled differently and have different meanings are called homonyms (*beet* and *beat; brake* and *break*).

Day 1
Pretest and Word Lists

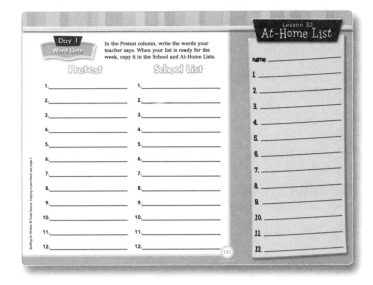

Before Photocopy the Answer Key/ Shopping List page (page 156 in this Teacher's Edition) for each student.

During Say each pair of words in bold, read the context sentence, and repeat the words. Have students record the pretest words in the pretest column on page 125 of the Student Book. Remind students to write two words for each sentence (and three words for number 10).

After Distribute to students a copy of the Answer Key/Shopping List page so that they can correct their pretests.

- Students should cross out any misspelled words and write the correct spelling. Consider a pair wrong if one word was misspelled. Word pairs that were correctly spelled can be replaced with pairs from the Shopping List. (See note below.)

- Be sure that each student has a list of six word pairs, which they should copy into the School and At-Home Lists and the Sorting Boxes (page 156).

Pretest context sentences (spelling words in bold)

1. **Beat** some **beet** juice into mashed potatoes to make them pink.
2. If Henry presses the bicycle **brake** too hard, he may **break** it.
3. The seats on the **plane** were covered with **plain** fabric.
4. I **sent** Jimmy one **cent** as a funny birthday present.
5. The farmers **heard** the **herd** of cows mooing.
6. **Their** coats are over **there**!
7. The only time there is **peace** in our kitchen is when everyone has a **piece** of pizza.
8. Since he could not find his baton, the conductor **led** the band using a **lead** pencil.
9. I **ate** dinner at **eight** o'clock.
10. **By** the way, did you **buy** Jon a going away gift before he says **bye** to us?
11. Because of the heavy **mist**, I **missed** the chance to look at the solar eclipse.
12. **No**, I do not **know** the solution to this math problem.

At-Home List Send the At-Home List home so that families can use the following activities with their students: word hunt, flashcards, more homonyms.

NOTE The Shopping List provides words below grade level (the first four rows), at grade level (the middle four rows), and above grade level (the last four rows).

Name _____

Answer Key

1. beat/beet
2. brake/break
3. plane/plain
4. sent/cent
5. heard/herd
6. their/there
7. peace/piece
8. led/lead
9. ate/eight
10. by/buy/bye
11. mist/missed
12. no/know

Shopping List

for/four/fore	already/all ready
where/wear	side/sighed
great/grate	bin/been
way/weigh	some/sum
son/sun	toe/tow
shoe/shoo	steal/steel
your/you're	threw/through
oh/owe	wood/would
tail/tale	to/too/two
weather/whether	principal/principle
week/weak	pole/poll
capitol/capital	build/billed

Sorting Boxes

Day 2
Word Sorting

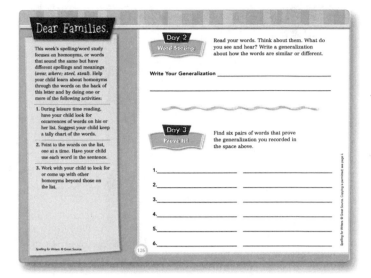

Have students look at the words carefully. Then have them decide for themselves a way or ways in which they can sort the words (do an open sort). Once they have made their sorts, have them write a generalization about the words.

- After students do an open sort, bring the class together to come to a consensus. If students have not or cannot come to consensus, model for them a way to sort all the words. You can use oversized word cards (CD-ROM) or a cut-up transparency (Transparency 29) and overhead to facilitate your model.

- Guide students to discover that the words are homonym pairs, or words that sound the same but have different spellings and meanings.

- Show homonym pairs (*beat/beet, peace/piece*). Have students pronounce each word in the pair. Ask students what is the same about the words. Ask how the words differ. Help students state a generalization based in the activity: *Some words sound the same, but they have different spellings and meanings.*

- Have students write the generalization in their Student Book (page 126). You might also write the generalization on a sentence strip or poster to display for the duration of the lesson. Leave room for students to add some of their Prove It! words from Day 3.

- Have students store their Sorting Boxes. (See page xi in this Teacher's Edition.)

Day 3
Prove It!

Students should review the generalization: *Some words may sound the same, but they have different spellings and meanings.* Then send them off to find in readable materials more examples that prove the generalization to be true. Tell students that they must be able to read and pronounce any word they find and record for the activity. Adjust the amount and kind of reading material students will use and the number of words students should find, according to their needs. Keep the Prove It! lists to put in a class word bank or chart for future reference.

NOTE Students will probably not find a pair of homonyms in one place. They should look for a word that has a homonym and write both words.

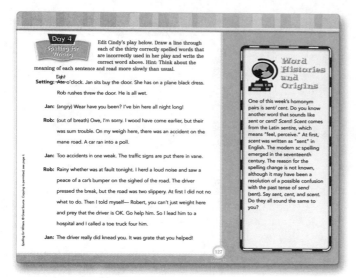

Have students edit Cindy's play. Tell students that when Cindy spell-checked her play on her computer, it had no errors. Students should find the <u>thirty</u> words that are spelled correctly but are used incorrectly in the context of the play. Students can work in pairs.

Answers

Setting: ~~Ate~~ (eight) o'clock. Jan sits ~~buy~~ (by) the door. She has on a ~~plane~~ (plain) black dress. Rob rushes ~~threw~~ (through) the door. He is all wet.

Jan: (angrily) ~~Wear~~ (Where) have you been? I've ~~bin~~ (been) here all night long!

Rob: (out of breath) ~~Owe~~ (oh), I'm sorry. I ~~wood~~ (would) have come earlier, but ~~their~~ (there) was ~~sum~~ (some) trouble. On my ~~weigh~~ (way) here, there was an accident on the ~~mane~~ (main) road. A car ran into a ~~poll~~ (pole).

Jan: ~~Too~~ (Two) accidents in one ~~weak~~ (week). The traffic signs are put there in ~~vane~~ (vain).

Rob: Rainy ~~whether~~ (weather) was at fault tonight. I ~~herd~~ (heard) a loud noise and saw a ~~peace~~ (piece) of a car's bumper on the ~~sighed~~ (side) of the road. The driver pressed the ~~break~~ (brake), but the road was ~~two~~ (too) slippery. At first I did not ~~no~~ (know) what to do. Then I told myself—Robert, you can't just ~~weight~~ (wait) here and ~~prey~~ (pray) that the driver is OK. Go help him. So I ~~lead~~ (led) him to a hospital and I called a ~~toe~~ (tow) truck ~~four~~ (for) him.

Jan: The driver really did ~~knead~~ (need) you. It was ~~grate~~ (great) that you helped!

Proofreading Tip A spell checker on a computer will generally not identify incorrectly used homonyms. Humans sometimes have trouble spotting them, too, because they are spelled correctly! Remind students to read very slowly, pausing when they come to a word that can be spelled two ways to decide if it is the right spelling.

WORD HISTORY Students may be curious to know the origin of the word *cent*. Cent comes from the Latin *centum*, meaning "hundred." It first appeared in English in the form of *per cent*, originally used by the financier Sir Thomas Gresham (in 1568). The use of *cent* for a unit of currency dates from the 1780s, when it was adopted by the newly founded United States of America. Its status as one hundredth of a dollar was officially ordained by the Continental Congress on August 8, 1786.

Day 5
Word Play and Posttest

Have students try to make up "teakettle" sentences using their homonyms pairs. The idea is to substitute the word *teakettle* for each homonym within a sentence. When students have finished writing their sentences, have them trade sentences with their partner. Each partner tries to solve the "teakettle" sentence. Review the example in the Student Book, asking students which homonym pair is represented. Students should write their answers.

Answer: "<u>Where</u> in the world would you be if you had to <u>wear</u> snowshoes?"

Posttest Have students tear out the perforated posttest. Students should pair up with their buddies or partners and exchange School Lists (page 125 in the Student Book). Students take turns testing each other on their respective spelling words. Collect the posttest sheets and record the correct response percentages. Mastery is 10 out of 12 words correct, or 80%. For students who do not achieve posttest mastery, see page xv in this Teacher's Edition.

After the posttest, have students select one or two anchor words to help them remember the word feature in this lesson. Record the words on the "Anchor Words" poster and refer to them in the Review lesson.

Lesson 32
Posttest

name _____

1. _____
2. _____
3. _____
4. _____
5. _____
6. _____
7. _____
8. _____
9. _____
10. _____
11. _____
12. _____

128

Day 5
Word Play

Using as many homonym pairs as possible, create sentences that use the word "teakettle" in place of the two homonyms. After you write your "teakettle" sentences, trade your sentence(s) with a buddy for him or her to solve.

Example: Which homonyms belong in the following sentence?

"<u>Teakettle</u> in the world would you be if you had to <u>teakettle</u> snowshoes?"

_____
_____
_____
_____
_____
_____
_____
_____

Lesson 33

Dictionary Terms. There are words specific to certain reference sources, such as the dictionary (*guide words, definition*).

Day 1
Pretest and Word Lists

Before Photocopy the Answer Key (page 161 in this Teacher's Edition) for each student.

During Say each word in bold, read the context sentence, and repeat the word. Have students record the pretest words in the pretest column on page 129 of the Student Book.

After Distribute to students a copy of the Answer Key page so that they can correct their pretests.

- Students should cross out any misspelled words and write the correct spelling. Students can fill out their list with examples of the pretest words. For example, students could choose examples of guide words from a dictionary, pairs of synonyms or antonyms, or the names of the parts of speech. There is no Shopping List.

- Students should copy only the misspelled words into the School and At-Home Lists and the Sorting Boxes (page 161).

Pretest context sentences (spelling word in bold)

1. The **guide words** at the top of the dictionary page are the first and last words on the page.
2. A **definition** is the meaning of a word.
3. Some **spellings** of words are different from how they are pronounced.
4. All **syllables** include a vowel sound.
5. A **pronunciation key** shows how to say a word.
6. English has eight **parts of speech**, including nouns and verbs.
7. I couldn't figure out the word's meaning from the dictionary **entry**.
8. Is "whisper" an **antonym** of "yell"?
9. Can you think of a **synonym** for "difficult"?
10. The **word history** explains how a word came into the English language.
11. Syllables that are stressed get an **accent mark**.
12. Refer to a dictionary to find the **meaning** of a word.

At-Home List Send the At-Home List home so that families can use the following activities with their students: use a dictionary, guide word guesses, definitions.

Name _____

Answer Key

1. guide words

2. definition

3. spellings

4. syllables

5. pronunciation key

6. parts of speech

7. entry

8. antonym

9. synonym

10. word history

11. accent mark

12. meaning

Sorting Boxes

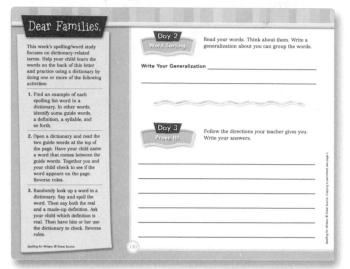

Day 2
Word Sorting

Look at all the lesson terms with students. Guide students to notice with you that the terms are specific to one kind of reference source and its use—the dictionary.

Talk briefly with students about several of the terms, encouraging them to help direct the discussion. Then have students do an open sort of the terms. Students can figure out their own ways to group the terms on their list. Start them off, as needed, by suggesting ways of sorting:

- most familiar/least familiar terms

- terms related to the sounds of words

- terms related to the meaning of words.

If students are unfamiliar with the terms, explain them. Having dictionaries available in the classroom is recommended. (Access to an online dictionary is helpful, too.)

Have students write a generalization about all their words in their Student Book (page 130): *The terms are specific to one kind of reference source and its use—the dictionary.* You might also write the generalization on a sentence strip or poster to display for the duration of the lesson. Leave room for students to add some of their Prove It words from Day 3. Have students store their Sorting Boxes. (See page xi in this Teacher's Edition.)

Students should review the generalization: *There are specific terms related to reference sources, such as the dictionary, and their use.* Then choose one of the following activities to enable students to prove the generalization.

Day 3
Prove It!

1. Have students look at the explanatory front matter in different dictionaries to confirm the importance and relevance of the spelling list terms to dictionary use.

2. Have students explore a different source, such as a thesaurus (explanatory front matter section), to find examples of terms specific to its use. Can students find any overlap with dictionary terms?

Make available the materials students will need for either or both activities. Keep the Prove It! lists to put in a class word bank or chart for future reference.

Day 4
Spelling for Writing

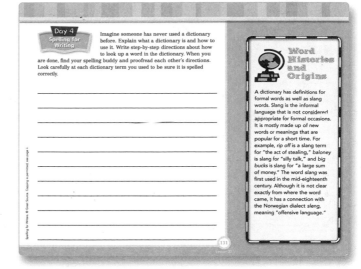

Have students write to explain what a dictionary is and how to use it. Students should include step-by-step directions on how to look up a word in the dictionary.

Proofreading Tip Offer these suggestions to students when they proofread their writing:

- Reread the directions to see if they make sense and comply with the directions.

- Make sure steps are sequenced correctly and numbered.

- Check capitalization and punctuation.

- Look carefully at each dictionary term to be sure it is spelled correctly.

WORD HISTORY Words make their way into standard English in a number of ways. One way is called *clipped forms*. Clipped forms are words that are shortened forms of polysyllabic words, such as *gas* for *gasoline* and *phone* for *telephone*. Challenge students to come up with the clipped forms of the words listed below and to be on the lookout for other clipped forms.

popular (pop)	airplane (plane)	necktie (tie)
gymnasium (gym)	referee (ref)	teenager (teen)
veterinarian (vet)	advertisement (ad)	automobile (auto)

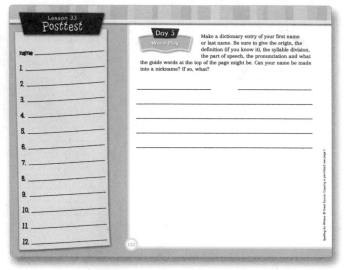

Have students make a dictionary entry
for their first or last name (or both). Tell
students to include the origin of their
name, the definition (if applicable), the
syllable division, the part of speech, the
pronunciation, and what the guide words
might be at the top of the page on which
their name appears.

Posttest Have students tear out the
perforated posttest. Students should pair up with their buddies or partners and
exchange School Lists (page 129 in the Student Book). Students take turns testing each
other on their respective spelling words. Collect the posttest sheets and record the correct response percentages. Mastery is 10 out of 12 words correct, or 80%. For students
who do not achieve posttest mastery, see page xv in this Teacher's Edition.

After the posttest, have students select one or two anchor words to help them remember the word feature in this lesson. Record the words on the "Anchor Words" poster
and refer to them in the Review lesson.

Lesson 34

Contractions. A contraction is two smaller words joined into one word so that it can be said more quickly (*I'll, aren't*). An apostrophe replaces missing letters.

Day 1
Pretest and Word Lists

Before Photocopy the Answer Key/ Shopping List page (page 166 in this Teacher's Edition) for each student.

During Say each word in bold, read the context sentence, and repeat the word. Have students record the pretest words in the pretest column on page 133 of the Student Book.

Day 1
Word Lists

In the Pretest column, write the words your teacher says. When your list is ready for the week, copy it in the School and At-Home Lists.

Pretest

1._____
2._____
3._____
4._____
5._____
6._____
7._____
8._____
9._____
10._____
11._____
12._____

School List

1._____
2._____
3._____
4._____
5._____
6._____
7._____
8._____
9._____
10._____
11._____
12._____

Lesson 34
At-Home List

name _____

1. _____
2. _____
3. _____
4. _____
5. _____
6. _____
7. _____
8. _____
9. _____
10. _____
11. _____
12. _____

After Distribute to students a copy of the Answer Key/Shopping List page so that they can correct their pretests.

- Students should cross out any misspelled words and write the correct spelling. Words that were correctly spelled can be replaced with words from the Shopping List. Identify the list from which students should choose their words. (See below.)

- Be sure that each student has a list of twelve correctly spelled words, which they should copy into the School and At-Home Lists and the Sorting Boxes (page 166).

Pretest context sentences (spelling word in bold)

1. *I'll* be leaving the party soon.
2. I *haven't* had pizza in a while.
3. We *aren't* going to school today.
4. My dentist said that I *shouldn't* eat sweets.
5. *Who's* knocking on my door?
6. They *won't* allow any pets in the store.
7. *There's* a stain on the rug.
8. We *mustn't* make any noise in the library.
9. "*That's* hilarious!" cried the audience member.
10. Jane is so funny; *she'd* make anyone laugh out loud.
11. *They'll* find something to do in their spare time.
12. My teacher *isn't* teaching today because she is sick.

At-Home List Send the At-Home List home so that families can use the following activities with their students: word cards, listen for contractions.

NOTE The Shopping List provides words below grade level (first two rows), at grade level (middle two rows), and above grade level (last two rows).

Name _____

Answer Key

1. I'll	7. there's
2. haven't	8. mustn't
3. aren't	9. that's
4. shouldn't	10. she'd
5. who's	11. they'll
6. won't	12. isn't

Shopping List

I've	they've	it's	you'll
we've	doesn't	hasn't	don't
he'll	we're	who'd	she's
it's	they're	she'll	we'll
weren't	wasn't	you're	he'll
where's	let's	he'd	you've

Sorting Boxes

Day 2
Word Sorting

Have students look at the words carefully. Then have them decide for themselves a way or ways in which they can sort the words (do an open sort). Once they have made their sorts, have them write a generalization about the words.

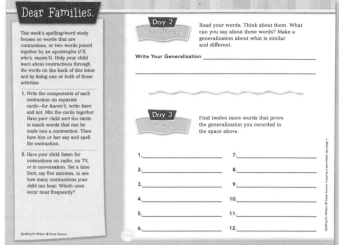

- After students do an open sort, bring the class together to come to a consensus. If students have not or cannot come to consensus, model for them a way to sort all the words. You can use oversized word cards (CD-ROM) or a cut-up transparency (Transparency 31) and overhead to facilitate your model.

- Guide students to discover that all the words are contractions, or two words joined together by an apostrophe so they can be said more quickly.

- Students' general categories for the sorting should reflect the second word that forms the contraction. For example, you might focus on words that are contractions with *not*.

- After students successfully make their sorts, they should realize that the number of letters replaced by the apostrophe in the contraction varies depending on the second word. For example, *have* and *not* become *haven't*, of which only the *o* is missing. However, *she* and *would* form *she'd*, in which the apostrophe replaces *w, o, u,* and *l*.

- Point out that some contractions have different meanings. The contraction *she'd* can be either "she had" or "she would."

- Have students write the generalization in their Student Book (page 134). You might also write the generalization on a sentence strip or poster to display for the duration of the lesson. Leave room for students to add some of their Prove It! words from Day 3.

- Have students store their Sorting Boxes. (See page xi in this Teacher's Edition.)

Students should review the generalization: *All the words are contractions, or two words joined together by an apostrophe so they can be said more quickly.* Then send them off to find in readable materials more examples that prove the generalization to be true. Tell students that they must be able to read and pronounce any word they find and record for the activity. Adjust the amount and kind of reading material students will use and the number of words they should find, according to their needs. Keep the Prove It! lists to put in a class word bank or chart for future reference.

NOTE Students might find possessive words, words that use apostrophes to show ownership. Explain the difference and refocus students on contractions.

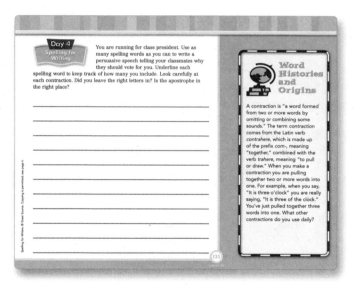

The goal of any spelling program is for students to be able to use their words in writing. Have each student write a persuasive speech telling classmates why they should vote for him or her as the next class president. Students should underline their words to help them keep track of how many they are able to include. Point out that contractions are not usually used in formal writing but are acceptable in informal writing, especially dialogue.

Remind students of the elements of a persuasive speech:

- The speech should highlight the writer's qualities as a president (including what problems they will solve and what things they will do in the future).

- Punctuation should convey the writer's emotions.

Proofreading Tip Students should focus their attention on any words in their writing that use an apostrophe. They should examine each word to be sure that, if the word is a contraction, the correct letters have been left in the word and the apostrophe is in the correct place.

WORD HISTORY Tell students that there are four definitions for the word *contraction:* Definition 1: "a shortening or tensing of a muscle." Definition 2: "the process or result of becoming smaller or pressed together." Definition 3: "a word formed from two or more words by omitting or combining some sounds." Definition 4: "the act of decreasing (something) in size, volume, quantity or scope." Students should realize that the word *contraction* implies that something gets smaller, whether it is a muscle, a word, or an object.

Word Play and Posttest

Have student pairs play dominoes with their spelling and Prove It words. Students can use their Sorting Boxes or make new cards. Then they should pair up with their partner and mix all the words together. Each student gets half the pile of "dominoes." Students should try to match up as many words as possible. The student who correctly matches the most words wins. Words match if the last letter of the word is the same as the first letter of the next word. Keep a set of dominoes in a word study center or other accessible place for students to use in their spare time.

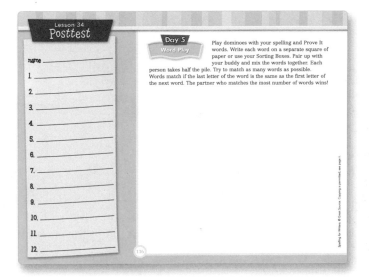

| where's | shouldn't | there's |

Posttest Have students tear out the perforated posttest. Students should pair up with their buddies or partners and exchange School Lists (page 133 in the Student Book). Students take turns testing each other on their respective spelling words. Collect the posttest sheets and record the correct response percentages. Mastery is 10 out of 12 words correct, or 80%. For students who do not achieve posttest mastery, see page xv in this Teacher's Edition. After the posttest, have students select one or two anchor words to help them remember the word feature in this lesson. Record the words on the "Anchor Words" poster and refer to them in the Review lesson.

Periodically, check writing samples from your students for transfer of the word features that have been taught. The features for the last three lessons are as follows:

Lesson 32: Homonyms
Lesson 33: Dictionary Terms
Lesson 34: Contractions

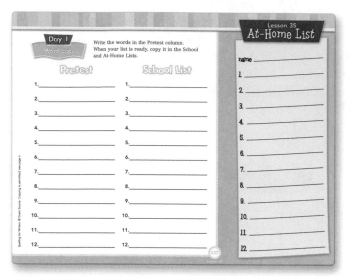

Day 1
Pretest and Word Lists

Before There are three options for selecting the pretest words. Choose the one most appropriate for your students.

1. Have students think of two words that fit the spelling pattern and write them.

2. Use the words that you and your class collected on the "Anchor Words" poster.

3. Use the examples given below.

If you will dictate the words, either from the "Anchor Words" poster or from below, write them on a copy of the Answer Key page (Teacher's Edition page 171). Photocopy the filled-in Answer Key page for each student.

During Announce each word feature. Then state the spelling generalization and give the words or tell students to think of two words. Students will write two pretest words for each feature (except 4 and 6) on page 137 of the Student Book.

After If you dictated the words, distribute a copy of the Answer Key so that students can self-correct their pretests. Otherwise, correct students' pretests.

- For any word feature that students got correct, send them back to the lesson for that feature to select a word from their Prove It! list they want to learn to spell.

- Be sure that each student has a list of correctly spelled words, which they should copy into the School and At-Home Lists and the Sorting Boxes.

Word Features and Generalizations

1. **Prefixes and Suffixes.** Some words can have both a prefix and a suffix, as in *immovable* and *uneventful*. (*Lesson 28*)

2. **Doubled Consonants (at syllable juncture).** When part of a word follows the VCCV pattern, it should be divided into syllables between the doubled consonant, as in *flammable* and *current*. (*Lesson 29*)

3. **Irregular Plurals.** Plural forms of some words are irregular, as are *data* and *knives*. (*Lesson 30*)

(continued on page 172)

Name _____

Answer Key

1. _____ (*Lesson 28*)
2. _____ (*Lesson 28*)
3. _____ (*Lesson 29*)
4. _____ (*Lesson 29*)
5. _____ (*Lesson 30*)
6. _____ (*Lesson 30*)
7. _____ (*Lesson 31*)
8. _____ (*Lesson 32*)
9. _____ (*Lesson 32*)
10. _____ (*Lesson 33*)
11. _____ (*Lesson 34*)
12. _____ (*Lesson 34*)

Sorting Boxes

4. **Compound Words**. A compound word is formed when two words come together to make a new word, as in *worthwhile*. (*Lesson 31*)

5. **Homonyms**. Homonyms sound the same but have different spellings and meanings, as in *heard* and *herd*. (*Lesson 32*)

6. **Dictionary Terms**. Some terms are specific to one kind of reference source, such as the dictionary: for example, *antonym*. (*Lesson 33*)

7. **Contractions**. A contraction is two words joined together; an apostrophe replaces the missing letters, as in *who's* and *mustn't*. (*Lesson 34*)

At-Home List Send the At-Home List home so that families can use the following activities with their children: word sorting, word hunt, word-guessing game.

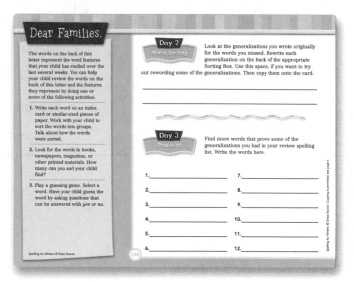

Students work with partners to revisit the generalizations for words they misspelled on the Pretest. Suggest that they look back at the generalizations they wrote in their book at time of initial study of the lesson's words. Tell them to try to reword the generalizations to help them better remember them. Even students who got all the words correct can revisit and reword several generalizations that were unclear the first time.

The rewording process should provide students insight into what "rules" govern many different sets of words. Students should rewrite their revised generalizations on the backs of their Sorting Boxes.

As a closing step, have students work in pairs to sort their words into groups that make sense. Circulate through the room to talk with students about their word sorts. The explanations of the sorts tell you what students understand about words.

After students revisit and revise the several generalizations for this week's review, send them off to find in readable materials more examples that prove as many of the generalizations as possible. Tell students that they must be able to read and

pronounce any word they find and record for the activity. Adjust the amount and kind of reading material students will use and the number of words they should find, according to their needs. Keep the Prove It! lists to put in a class word bank or chart for future reference.

Day 4
Spelling for Writing

Tell students to look at their list of spelling words and use as many of them as possible to write a story. Students can also include words from the word hunt (Prove It!). Sentences should be constructed carefully so that words are explained in context.

Tell students that

- the words they choose will help determine the content of their stories.

- all stories have a beginning, a middle, and an ending.

- dialogue helps the reader know what the characters are like and adds interest to the story.

- the sentences that contain spelling words must clearly convey the meaning of each spelling word used.

Proofreading Tip Remind students once again that reading and proofreading are different. Ask students to share which proofreading strategies they use and which ones are most helpful. Some of the strategies they might mention are the following: read for one item at a time, touch each word with a pencil point, read the words aloud, look for errors the writer commonly makes, and work with a partner.

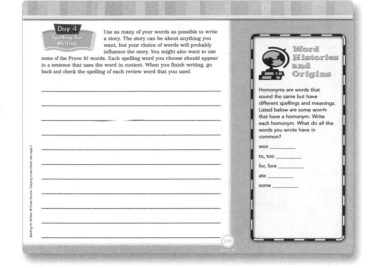

> **Word Histories and Origins** Students are reminded that homonyms are words that sound the same but have different meanings. They are then asked to write the homonyms for the listed words. All the words that students are to write have something in common: They are all words used in math.

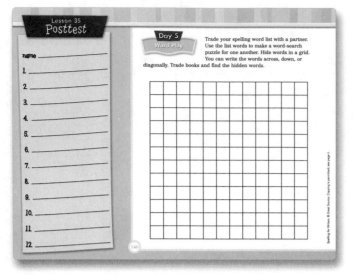

Have students swap spelling lists and create a word find for each other. Words should be hidden in a grid and can be placed so they can be read horizontally, vertically, or diagonally. Once the words are in place, students should fill the grid with random letters that do not form words. Once the word searches are ready, have the partners trade books and find the hidden words.

Other activities that students can do to review the words include the following:

• Have students choose a set of Sorting Boxes from a previous week and time themselves when they sort the cards. Students should sort the cards several times to improve their sorting time. (Copy Masters of the pretest words can be found in the Transparencies and Copy Masters folder. Or, generate word cards from the CD-ROM.)

• Students can use their review list to play one of the Word Play games from a previous lesson: for example, "Hangman," "Hit or Miss," or "Bull's Eye." They could also make a crossword puzzle.

• Generate a practice activity from the CD-ROM.

Posttest Have students carefully tear out the posttest form on the Student Book page 140. Students should pair up with their buddies or partners and exchange School Lists (page 137 in the Student Book). Students take turns testing each other on their respective spelling words. Collect the posttest sheets and correct them. Mastery is 80% of the number of words they had for the week (10 correct out of 12). For students who do not achieve posttest mastery, see page xi in this Teacher's Edition.

Days 1-2
Word Lists

Before Have students locate page 141 in the Student Book on which they will record the spelling words.

During Say each word in boldface (page 176) aloud. The word features are identified in parentheses for your convenience. These words were specifically chosen because they represent grade level words for a given feature. If you substituted other words, use them here. It is recommended that this assessment be administered over two to five days, in short intervals, in order to best meet the needs of your students and to avoid student fatigue. On Days 3-5, if the assessment is still ongoing, students can continue with the other activities after you administer a small portion of the assessment.

After Interpret students' responses, analyzing first their successes in spelling a word that meets the word feature criterion and then taking a hard look at where they may have miscued, perhaps recalling a different word feature and misapplying it. We suggest you do not mark in the Student Book. A record sheet is provided (see page 179 in this Teacher's Edition). This records the features and allows you to document growth for each student. It is important for students not to see the markings, so simply transfer any attempts to the record sheet. This reinforces the understanding that *Spelling for Writers* developmentally supports the spelling strategies that students bring to their writing, rather than focusing on mastery of whole words. As you will notice, the students' profile easily documents growth.

Days 1-2
Word Lists

In the columns, write the words your teacher says.

Benchmark Assessment

1._____   13._____
2._____   14._____
3._____   15._____
4._____   16._____
5._____   17._____
6._____   18._____
7._____   19._____
8._____   20._____
9._____   21._____
10._____   22._____
11._____   23._____
12._____   24._____

141

Dear Families,

Your child has taken the last of three benchmark assessments in the spelling program, *Spelling for Writers*. The purpose of the assessments was to provide an overall picture of students' developing knowledge of the word features (patterns and structures of words) taught this year.

Benchmark assessments were also administered in lessons 1 and 20 of *Spelling for Writers*. The benchmark words were carefully selected to reflect each child's current knowledge of certain word features. Mastery is not expected and grades are not given. Rather, the benchmark assessments are a tool for planning instruction.

(continued)

Benchmark Assessment This assessment tool measures students' growth and development in the spelling process. Do not make substitutions for boldfaced words.

1. **acid** (short vowel)
2. **button** (short vowel in 2-syllable words)
3. **angry** (long vowels, final *y*)
4. **chase** (*e* marker)
5. **mule** (*e* marker)
6. **close** (*e* marker)
7. **dime** (*e* marker)
8. **Pete** (*e* marker)
9. **avenue** (long vowels, silent letter pattern)
10. **doubtful** (consonant, silent letter pattern)
11. **southerner** (*r*-controlled vowels)
12. **snowbound** (diphthong)
13. **studios** (plurals)
14. **done** (irregular past-tense)
15. **withhold** (compound words)
16. **wrapping** (doubling before ending or suffix)
17. **uncommon** (prefix)

18. **painless** (suffix)
19. **angel/angelic** (derivations and relations)
20. **slammed** (blends)
21. **lovelier/loveliest** (comparatives)
22. **threw/through** (homonyms)
23. **taught** (complex vowel pattern)
24. **launch** (preconsonant nasals)
25. **knee/knelt** (vowel alternations)
26. **accurate** (doubling at syllable juncture)
27. **odor** (*r*-controlled in more complex words)
28. **incorrect** (prefixes and meanings)
29. **connect** (doubling at syllable juncture)
30. **undoable** (prefix/suffix in the same word)
31. **oxen** (irregular plurals)
32. **shoreline** (compound words)
33. **missed/mist** (homonyms)
34. **wouldn't** (contractions)

Letter to the Families

On pages 141-142 of the Student Book, there is a letter addressed to your students' families. The letter explains in a brief way the purpose of the last of three benchmark assessments: examining the student's responses enabled you to assess the student's skills development.

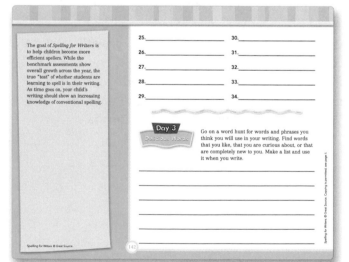

Day 3
Delicious Words

If students are still taking the benchmark assessment, administer more of the words before students begin the word-hunt activity. Continue to encourage your students' interest in words by having them search for more "delicious" words that will enhance their personal writing. You might also want to have students revisit the words they found in lessons 1 and 20, sharing words that still stand out as favorites. Record words on the "Delicious Words" poster.

Day 4
Spelling for Writing

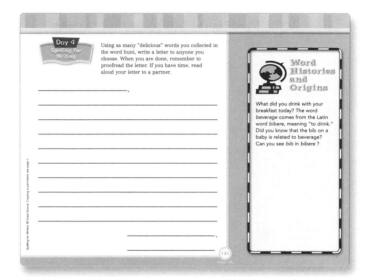

The goal of any spelling program is for students to be able to use their words in writing. Encourage students to use some of their newfound words from the word hunt to write a letter.

Tell students to remember that

- a letter should include the five basic parts: heading, greeting, body, closing, and signature.

- the tone will depend on the purpose and audience of the letter: formal if writing to someone they have never met or informal if writing to a friend.

- commas should be used appropriately in the heading, greeting, and closing as well as the body.

Proofreading Tip Reading aloud is a good strategy for proofreading. Hearing the words helps the writer notice whether all the words have been included and whether the punctuation is accurate.

Word History Students are introduced to the word *beverage* and told a little about its history. On Student Book page 144, students are asked to find out how some beverages were named. Some names may be obvious: for example, Silk® soy products were probably so-named because they are "as smooth as silk." Other names may require some research on the Internet or in the library.

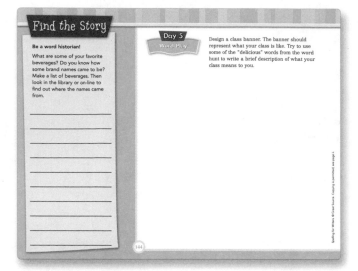

Have students create a class banner. Tell students that the banner should represent the entire class. Remind students to include a brief description of what their class means to them. Encourage students to use as many "delicious" or spelling list words as possible.

Name_____

Benchmark Assessment Chart

Word and Feature	Lesson 1	Lesson 18	Lesson 36
1. **acid** (short vowel)			
2. **button** (short vowel)			
3. **angry** (y ending with a vowel sound)			
4. **chase** (e-marker)			
5. **mule** (e-marker)			
6. **close** (e-marker)			
7. **dime** (e-marker)			
8. **Pete** (e-marker)			
9. **avenue** (vowel silent letter pattern)			
10. **doubtful** (consonant silent letter pattern)			
11. **southerner** (r-controlled vowel)			
12. **snowbound** (diphthong)			
13. **studios** (plural)			
14. **done** (irregular past-tense)			
15. **withhold** (compound word)			
16. **wrapping** (doubling before ending or suffix)			
17. **uncommon** (prefix)			
18. **painless** (suffix)			
19. **angel/angelic** (derivations and relations)			
20. **slammed** (blend)			
21. **lovelier/loveliest** (comparative/superlative)			
22. **threw/through** (homonyms)			
23. **taught** (complex vowel pattern)			
24. **launch** (preconsonant nasal)			
25. **knee/knelt** (vowel alternations)			
26. **accurate** (doubling at syllable juncture)			
27. **odor** (r-controlled vowel)			
28. **incorrect** (prefix)			
29. **connect** (doubling at syllable juncture)			
30. **undoable** (prefix/suffix in the same word)			
31. **oxen** (irregular plurals)			
32. **shoreline** (compound words			
33. **missed/mist** (homonyms)			
34. **wouldn't** (contractions)			

Class Record Chart

Student	2	3	4	5	6	7	8	9	10	11	12	13	14	15	16

Student	17	18	21	22	23	24	25	26	28	29	30	31	32	33	34

See the reteaching ideas on Teacher's Edition page xi for students who do not achieve 80% on the posttest..

Word Features and Generalizations in *Spelling for Writers*

Lesson 2: Short Vowels. Every word in English has at least one vowel phoneme. These words have short vowel sounds: *drag, kept, grip, odd,* and *luck.*

Lesson 3: Short Vowels (two-syllable words). The words in this lesson all have at least one short vowel sound. Examples are *access, export,* and *drizzle.*

Lesson 4: Long Vowels (final *y*). When a long vowel sound comes at the end of a word or syllable, it probably ends in y (*supply*) or a vowel plus y (*repay*).

Lesson 5: Long Vowels (*e* marker). When a word ends with a silent e, the vowel closest to the silent e represents a long vowel sound. Examples are *fade, shine,* and *globe.*

Lesson 6: Long Vowels (silent letter patterns). Sometimes vowel letters make a pattern in which one vowel is long and one is silent, as in *beast, float, paint,* and *elbow.*

Lesson 7: Silent Consonant Patterns. Consonant letters can make a pattern in which one is silent, for example *tomb, knife,* and *gnaw.*

Lesson 8: *R*-Controlled Vowels. When r follows a vowel, the r influences, or controls, the vowel sound. Examples are *pillar, germs, thirty,* and *motor.*

Lesson 9: Diphthongs. Two side-by-side vowels can represent a sound that is neither short nor long. Examples are *moist, gown, loyal,* and *pound.*

Lesson 10: Plurals (-s, -es, *y* to *i*). Add –s to form the plural of most words (*rockets*). Add –es to words that end with *ch, x, s,* or *sh* (*arches*). Change *y* to *i* before adding –es (*berries*).

Lesson 11: Past Tense. The past-tense verbs in this lesson represent three sounds but only two spellings (*kept, whined, supported*).

Lesson 12: Compound Words. A compound word is made by putting two words together: *background, whenever,* and *storybook.*

Lesson 13: Doubled Consonants (before endings). When the base word has one short vowel sound and ends in a consonant, the consonant is doubled before adding the ending or suffix.

Lesson 14: Prefixes and Suffixes. When a prefix or suffix is added to a word, the meaning of the word changes (*unable, playful*).

Lesson 15: Derivations and Relations. Words that are related may sound different but are similar in spelling (*reduce/reduction*).

Lesson 16: Consonant Blends. When a consonant comes before l or r, the sounds are blended together (*blade, grapes*).

Lesson 17: Comparatives and Superlatives. Endings are added to words to show comparison of different numbers of objects. Sometimes a spelling change is required (*louder, busiest*).

Lesson 18: Homonyms. These are words that sound the same but are spelled differently and have different meanings (*wear, where*).

Lesson 21: Complex Vowel Patterns. Two vowels together can stand for a vowel sound that is neither short nor long (*appl<u>au</u>d, f<u>ou</u>ght, cr<u>aw</u>l*).

Lesson 22: Preconsonant Nasals. The letters *m* and *n* are nasal consonants. When they come before another consonant, they are called preconsonant nasals, as in *chomp* and *belong*.

Lesson 23: Vowel Alternations. When an ending is added to a word, the vowel sound can change, although the spelling is preserved, as in *wide* and *width*.

Lesson 24: Doubled Consonants (at syllable juncture). Words are divided into syllables between double consonants: for example, *swim•ming* and *ap•pear*.

Lesson 25: *R*-Controlled Vowels. When a vowel is followed by *r,* the *r* influences (or controls) the sound of the vowel, as in *scar* and *author*.

Lesson 26: Prefixes (same base word or root). A prefix changes the meaning of a base word or root, as shown by these word pairs that have the same base or root but a different prefix (*deflate, inflate*).

Lesson 28: Prefixes and Suffixes. Prefixes and suffixes change the meaning of a word. Sometimes a word has both a prefix and a suffix (*disabled, unwinding*).

Lesson 29: Doubled Consonants (at syllable juncture). When a word follows the VCCV pattern, syllables are divided between the two consonants, as in *flam•mable*.

Lesson 30: Irregular Plurals. Plural words are formed in different ways (*knives, teeth*). Some words do not change when they are used as a plural (*deer*).

Lesson 31: Compound Words. A compound word is made up of separate words that come together to make a new word that has its own meaning (*alongside, bee-hive*).

Lesson 32: Homonyms. Words that sound the same but are spelled differently and have different meanings are called homonyms (*beet* and *beat*; *brake* and *break*).

Lesson 33: Dictionary Terms. There are words specific to certain reference sources, such as the dictionary (*guide words, definition*).

Lesson 34: Contractions. A contraction is two smaller words joined into one word to that it can be said more quickly (*I'll, aren't*). An apostrophe replaces missing letters.

Spelling for Writers: Foundation in Research

Spelling for Writers is rooted in research that examines instructional methods and the developmental aspects of learning to spell. Spelling instruction has a long history in the United States. In the late 1700s, spellers were shipped from England or reprinted in America. The instructional method mimicked those used in England, where learning the alphabet and then combinations of letters prepared students to learn 180 syllables (Hodges, 1977). Learning to spell was followed by learning to read.

In 1839, Horace Mann claimed the whole word method was "the superior spelling method" (Hodges, 1977, p.4). He suggested utilizing a memorization approach (Hodges, 1977). The spelling bee became a popular activity in many communities.

In Joseph Rice's influential 1897 article, "The Futility of the Spelling Grind," an analysis of 33,000 U.S. students' spelling achievement was presented (Hodges, 1977). His work found that outside influences—such as age, home, or school environment—had little effect on achievement. Therefore, he recommended that students spend 15 minutes per day in spelling study, and the words studied should be carefully selected based on orthographic features and difficulty (Hodges, 1977). Rice's research shaped studies about spelling instruction into the next century. Then, in the 1950s, a new scientific inquiry called "linguistics" emerged. Linguists studied the English language and discovered that it was not as irregular as previously thought. This finding suggested that teaching students to understand the patterns and features of words would prove more powerful than memorization. However, spelling basals remained virtually unchanged – every student in a grade level got the same list of words to learn for the Friday test. Some basals attempted to provide for differentiation by having students that scored well on a pretest take additional "challenge" words. These students got more—not different— words to study.

While many linguists were constructing knowledge about the English language and figuring out how to best teach spelling, others focused on how students learn to spell. Read's (1971) landmark study of preschool children's invented spellings argued that their attempts were not random. Rather, he observed consistent and progressive changes in children's invented spellings over time. Relying on their operating knowledge of the language, the children's errors made sense. Beers and Henderson (1977) also found logical error patterns that changed both systematically and longitudinally (Henderson, 1987). This understanding of the developmental nature of how children learn to spell gradually began to inform classroom practice (Fresch, 2003, p.821).

Many researchers support the belief that spelling is a developmental process: All students progress through the same continuum, but some move along faster than others. Word and activity selection is suggested by such key educators as Cunningham and Hall (1994), Gentry (1981), Zutell (1996), Schlagal and Schlagal

(1992), and Bear, Invernezzi, Templeton and Johnston (2004). While these researchers suggest ways to meet the individual, developmental needs of students, much teacher organization and decision making is required to create instruction. *Spelling for Writers* uses the developmental research, the authors' direct work with students, and research on graded word lists to create a series that offers teachers an organized, research-based approach for meeting individual needs.

References

Bear, D., Invernizzi, M., Templeton, S., & Johnston, F. (2000). *Words their way: Word study for phonics, vocabulary, and spelling instruction* (2nd ed.). Upper Saddle River, NJ: Prentice Hall.

Beers, J. & Henderson, E. (1977). A study of developing orthographic concepts among first grade children. *Journal of Research in English, 11,* 133-148.

Cunningham, P. & Hall, D. (1994). *Making words: Multilevel, hands-on, developmentally appropriate spelling and phonics activities.* Parsippany, NJ: Good Apple.

Fresch, M.J. (2003). A national survey of spelling instruction: Investigating teachers' beliefs and practice. *Journal of Literacy Research,* 35, 819-848.

Gentry, R. (1981). Learning to spell developmentally. *The Reading Teacher*, 34, 378-381.

Henderson, E. (1987). *Learning to read and spell.* DeKalb, IL: Northern Illinois University Press.

Hodges, R.E. (1977). In Adam's fall: A brief history of spelling instruction in the United States. In H.A. Robinson (Ed.), *Reading and writing instruction in the United States: Historical trends* (pp.1-16). Newark, DE: International Reading Association.

Read, C. (1971). Pre-school children's knowledge of English phonology. *Harvard Educational Review,* 41, 1-34.

Schlagal, R.C. & Schlagal, J.H. (1992). The integral character of spelling: Teaching strategies for multiple purposes. *Language Arts*, 69, 418-424.

Templeton, S. (1983). Using the spelling/meaning connection to develop word knowledge in older students. *Journal of Reading*, 27, 8-14.

Zutell, J. (1996). The Directed Spelling Teaching Activity (DSTA): Providing an effective balance in word study instruction. *The Reading Teacher*, 50, 98-108.

Introducing *Spelling for Writers* to the Community

Open house is the perfect time to introduce *Spelling for Writers* to students' families and the larger community. By that time, the families will have received several letters from the first few lessons of the year. This is the teacher's opportunity to encourage families to support their student by reading the letter and trying to do some of the suggested activities. The families will see that they can still practice the words with their student, but now they have multiple ways to work with their children. Additionally, each letter provides ways for families to talk about more words than just what is on their list for the week.

At the Open House or other forum, engage families in a word-sorting activity. Few people can resist organizing a group of word cards left on the table! After families have sorted the cards, ask them to share how they grouped the words. The amount of word knowledge that is used while sorting words and sharing the results is key activity in *Spelling for Writers*.

Another Open House activity might be to tell the families that you would like them to think of how a word, such as *chauffeur*, is spelled. Ask them: *This is a word we hear and use but have rare occasion to write. What did you think about to spell the word?* They might have thought about the way the "sh" sound can be spelled, how the "r" at the end might be spelled since this is a person, and so on. They might have tried to visualize it. These are all aspects of being a good speller: Good spellers use what they know about the language and their past experiences with words. This is what *Spelling for Writers* aims to do, provide students with a number of dependable strategies for independent writing.

When families have personal experience with the program and understand its purpose and approach, they are more likely to work with their children to support their spelling growth.

Suggested Resources for Spelling and Word Study

Almond, J. (1985). *Dictionary of Word Origins*. Secaucus, NJ: Citadel Press.

Barnette, M. (1997). *Ladyfingers and Nun's Tummies*. NY: Vintage Books.

Bear, D., Templeton, S., Invernizzi, M. & Johnston, F. (2004). *Words Their Way: Word Study for Phonics, Vocabulary and Spelling Instruction* (third edition). Columbus: Merrill.

Blevins, W. (1998). *Phonics from A to Z*. NY: Scholastic.

Bolton, F. and D. Snowball (1993). *Teaching Spelling: A Practical Resource*. Portsmouth, NH: Heinemann.

Bolton, F. and D. Snowball (1993). *Teaching Spelling: A Practical Resource*. Portsmouth, NH: Heinemann.

Branreth, G. (1988). *The Word Book*. London: Robson Books.

Bryson, B. (1990). *The Mother Tongue*. New York: William Morrow and Company.

Cunningham, P. & Hall, D. (1994). *Making Words*. Parsippany, NJ: Good Apple, Inc.

Ericson, L. & Juliebö, M. (1998). *The Phonological Awareness Handbook for Kindergarten and Primary Teachers*. Newark, DE: International Reading Association.

Flavel, L & R. (1992). *Dictionary of Idioms*. London: Kyle Cathie Ltd.

Fresch, M. J. & Wheaton, A. (1997). Sort, search and discover: Spelling in the child-centered classroom. *The Reading Teacher*, 51, 20-31.

Fresch, M. J. & Wheaton, A. (2002). *Teaching and Assessing Spelling: A Practical Approach that Strikes the Balance Between Whole-Group and Individualized Instruction*. NY: Scholastic.

Fresch, M. J. & Wheaton, A. (2004). *The Spelling List and Word Study Resource Book*. NY: Scholastic.

Funk, W. (1950). *Word Origins*. New York: Wings Books.

Ganske, K. (2000). *Word Journeys*. NY: Guilford Press.

Gentry, J. R. (2004). *The Science of Spelling*. Portsmouth, NH: Heinemann.

Goodman, K. (1993). *Phonics Phacts*. Jefferson City, MO: Scholastic.

Hanson, J. (1972). *Homographs: Words That Look the Same*. Minneapolis, MN: Lerner Publications.

Henderson, E. (1990). *Teaching Spelling, 2nd Edition*. Boston: Houghton Mifflin.

Henderson, E. and Beers, J. W. (Eds.) (1980). *Developmental and Cognitive Aspects of Learning to Spell: A Reflection of Word Knowledge*. Newark, DE: International Reading Association.

Henry, M.A, (2003). *Effective Decoding and Spelling Instruction*. Baltimore, MD: Brookes.

Hoad, T. F. (1993). *Concise Oxford Dictionary of English Etymology*. New York: Oxford University Press.

Hodges, R. E. (1981). *Learning to Spell*. Urbana, IL: National Council of Teachers of English.

Hughes, M. & Searle, D. (1997). *The Violent E and Other Tricky Sounds: Learning to Spell from Kindergarten through Grade 6.* York, ME: Stenhouse.

Jones, C. F. (1999). *Eat Your Words: A Fascinating Look at the Language of Food.* Illustrated by J. O'Brien. NY: Delacorte Press.

Jones, C. F. (1991). *Mistakes That Worked.* NY: Doubleday.

Kennedy, J. (1996). *Word Stems: A Dictionary.* New York: Soho Press.

Lederer, R. (1990). *Crazy English.* New York: Pocket Books.

Powell, D. & Hornsby, D. (1993). *Learning Phonics and Spelling in a Whole Language Classroom.* Jefferson City, MO: Scholastic.

Merriam-Webster New Book of Word Histories. (1991). Springfield, MA: Merriam-Webster, Inc.

Room, A. (1986). *The Fascinating Origins of Everyday Words.* Chicago: NTC Publishing.

Shipley, J. (1945). *Dictionary of Word Origins* New York: Dorset Press.

Stowe, C. M. (1996). *Spelling Smart!* West Nyack, NY: Center for Applied Research in Education.

Terban, M. (1996). *Dictionary of Idioms.* NY: Scholastic.

Tompkins, G. and Yaden, D. (1986). *Answering Students' Questions about Words.* Urbana, IL: National Council of Teacher's of English

Traupman, J. C. (1995). *Latin and English Dictionary.* New York: Bantam Books.

Venezky, R. (1999). *The American Way of Spelling: The Structure and Origin of American English Orthography.* NY: Guilford Press.

Wagstaff, J. (1993). *Phonics That Work.* Jefferson City, MO: Scholastic.

White, R. (1994). *An Avalanche of Anoraks.* New York: Crown Trade Paperbacks.

Wilde, S. (1997). *What's a Schwa Sound Anyway? A Holistic Guide to Phonetics, Phonics, and Spelling.* Portsmouth, N.H.: Heinemann.

Young, S. (1994). *Rhyming Dictionary.* New York: Scholastic.

Zutell, J. (1996). The directed spelling teaching activity (DSTA): Providing an effective balance in word study instruction. *The Reading Teacher, 50, 98-108.*

Word List (grade 4) Boldfaced words are pretest words.

abler	arches	birdbath	**busiest**	**chose**	corner
absent	**aren't**	birthday	**businessmen**	circle	corners
absolute	arrowhead	**blacksmith**	butterfly	**circuit**	**couch**
accent mark	aspect	**blade**	**buy**	circus	**country**
accepted	**assertive**	blank	**by**	cities	**countryman**
access	asset	**blanket**	bye	**clammy**	**courthouse**
accomplished	**ate**	bleacher	**bylaw**	**clapped**	crack
accomplishments	athlete	blind	**cacti**	clashed	cracked
acid	athletic	blizzard	**calves**	clause	**crawl**
activity	auction	block	cameras	claw	crawling
actor	**author**	blockade	camp	clay	crayon
afraid	**authority**	blonde	campfire	**clean**	**crazier**
afterthought	autocracy	blood	**cancellation**	cleanest	**creak**
agent	**autumn**	blossom	candid	clerk	creek
agreeable	**awesome**	blouse	cannot	**clever**	crew
airline	awful	blow	**capital**	climb	cricket
airplane	axes	**blubber**	**capitol**	**cloak**	**crisp**
align	babies	**bluff**	careful	**cloths**	criteria
alike	backbone	blushes	careless	cloud	**critic**
allergy	**background**	boar	cash	**clown**	crook
allowable	baked	boil	**caught**	**clumsiest**	crops
allowed	balloons	**boldface**	cauliflower	**coastline**	**cross**
along	barber	bother	**caulk**	cobblestone	**crosses**
alongside	**barge**	bought	cause	**code**	**crowd**
already	baseball	**bounce**	**causeway**	**coffeepot**	crowded
always	basketball	boxes	**caution**	coin	crumb
angel	bathroom	bragged	**cavity**	**cologne**	crystal
angelic	beacon	**bragging**	cent	colorful	**cunning**
angle	**beast**	**brain**	**central**	**comb**	**curlier**
angles	**beat**	brake	**centrality**	comedian	**current**
another	beat	branches	**chairperson**	comedy	customs
antibacterial	because	**braver**	**champ**	**comet**	cypress
antislavery	**beehive**	**brawny**	channels	**commitment**	dainty
antonym	been	**break**	charge	common	danced
anything	**beet**	brittle	chatter	**communities**	**data**
anyway	**befriend**	broadcast	**checkerboard**	commute	**daughter**
appear	**beggar**	broke	cheerleader	**companies**	dawn
appearance	beginning	brothers-in-law	**children**	**compose**	daytime
appeared	**belong**	**brush**	chill	**composition**	**dazzling**
applaud	**berries**	**build**	**chipmunk**	compressed	**debt**
applauded	biggest	bunch	chirp	concrete	decay
applause	**billed**	**burrow**	**chomp**	cork	deceased
apply	bin	**bushes**	**chopped**	corncob	**decide**

decision
declaration
declare
declared
decoy
deduct
deer
define
definition
definition
deflate
defray
defy
democracy
depressed
derailed
descendant
design
devise
different
dipper
dirtier
dirtiest
disabled
disappear
disappoint
disorganize
disrepair
ditch
divide
dividend
dock
doesn't
dollar
don't
doubt
down
downstairs
drag
dragged
drawing
dreamy
drizzle
dromedary

drummer
dull
dumb
dump
dusk
dwarves
dying
eagle
earthquake
easier
editor
editorial
eggplant
eight
either
elbow
elves
ember
enchant
enjoyable
entertainment
entry
envelope
envoy
estate
everybody
everyone
everywhere
exceed
exit
explain
explanation
explore
export
export
extreme
extremity
extrovert
eyelid
factories
fade
fancier
fare
farewell

favorite
finest
firecracker
firemen
fish
fitter
fixed
fjord
flakier
flammable
flashlight
flatter
flirted
float
foci
foil
folklore
followed
follower
for
fore
foreign
forethought
forever
forewarned
forty
fought
four
fresher
frown
froze
fulfilling
fume
funnier
funniest
furthermore
gallons
garbage
geese
gentler
germs
gift
giggle
giraffe

glance
glare
glass
glasses
glaze
glimpse
glitter
glittering
globe
gloomy
glossary
glove
glowing
glue
gnarl
gnat
gnaw
gnome
gnu
golf
gown
grabbed
graceful
grandmother
grapefruit
grapes
grapple
grate
great
Greece
greed
griddle
grinned
grinning
grip
grove
growth
guide words
gushed
hall
hallway
halves
hammer
handkerchief

happened
happiest
happily
hare
harm
hasn't
haul
haven't
hawk
he'd
he'll
hear
heard
heavier
heaviest
helpful
herd
here
hermit
highlands
hoard
hobbies
homesick
hooks
hopeful
hopped
horses
hospital
hospitality
howl
huge
hugging
humming
hurricane
hyperactive
hypoactive
I'll
I've
iced
ignite
ignition
illogical
immediately
immovable

imperfection
imply
import
inch
indent
indices
induct
inflatable
inflate
inland
insect
insects
inspect
install
installation
introvert
investment
invitation
invite
inward
isn't
it's
jammed
jaw
jogger
jolly
journeys
joyful
jump
June
just
kept
kick
kidded
kitties
knack
knapsack
knead
knee
kneel
knew
knife
knight
knit

knives
knob
knock
knoll
knothole
know
knowledge
knuckle
ladies
lair
lamb
launch
laundry
lead
league
leashes
leaves
led
let's
library
limb
list
literacy
littlest
loafer
loaves
locate
loiter
lonely
loud
louder
lounge
loveable
loves
lowlands
loyal
luck
luckiest
lullaby
lump
madder
main
major
majority

mane
March
marshes
marvelous
masterpiece
meaning
meddle
men
merriment
metal
metallic
mice
midday
mile
milky
million
mine
mischief
mischievous
missed
missing
mist
moist
monarchy
moonbeam
moose
morning
motor
mount
mouth
mower
mustn't
mute
nabbed
narrow
nastier
nation
national
natural
nature
need
newscast
no
noise

noisiest
notify
number
numerator
numerous
oatmeal
oblong
octopus
odd
oh
olive
onward
opportunities
orange
orchard
ordeal
other
ouch
our
overcome
overpriced
owe
oxen
oyster
painful
paint
parentheses
parties
parts of speech
party
passersby
patios
patted
pause
peace
peach
peaches
perfume
petted
pianos
picnic
piece
pillar
plain

plane
plank
planner
planning
playful
playground
plot
plum
plumber
plumbing
plump
plunked
point
poise
pole
poll
pollution
porch
pound
powder
practice
practiced
prank
pray
predict
prediction
prepaid
preschool
press
pretest
prey
price
pride
principal
principle
print
problem
proceed
produce
product
production
professor
pronunciation
key

proofread
proslavery
provide
provision
puppy
pushed
quicker
railroad
raining
raised
reaction
reappear
recall
recommendation
recopy
recreation
redirection
redo
reduce
reduction
refill
refuse
regroup
rely
removes
reorganize
repacked
repair
repay
replanted
reread
retell
retry
revise
revision
revoke
rhymed
ring
rises
robin
rockets
rubbed
runaway
saddened

sauce
scar
scared
scarf
scent
scout
screenplay
scribe
scrimmage
scrub
scuffled
seacoast
seashore
season
seaweed
segments
selves
semiclosed
semiskilled
send
sent
series
servant
setting
settle
shakiest
sharper
she'd
she'll
she's
shinbone
shine
shipping
shirt
shiver
shoe
shoo
shopper
shoreline
shouldn't
shout
shrank
shredding
shrimp

shy	sprung	survey	total	unlatched	**where**
side	spy	swamp	totality	unluckiest	**where's**
sighed	square	swimming	touchdown	**unnatural**	whereby
sign	**squirrel**	swung	tow	unoriginal	**whether**
sillier	stagecoach	**syllables**	town	**unplug**	**whined**
sirloin	**stake**	**synonym**	trade	unsafe	**whistled**
sister	stamp	**tagging**	transferred	**unstickable**	**whittle**
skate	**staunch**	tail	transmitter	unthinkable	who'd
skidded	steadier	tale	transplanted	untie	**who's**
skillful	**steak**	tallest	trapping	untouchable	**wide**
skimpy	steal	tapping	**tried**	unusual	widest
skipped	steel	taught	trimmed	**unwinding**	**width**
skipper	stepping	tease	**trough**	**urgent**	**windmill**
skunk	**stickier**	**teeth**	truck	**useful**	wives
slammed	**stink**	**televise**	**trump**	**usher**	women
slept	stone	**television**	trunk	**vacant**	**won't**
slope	stopped	**textbook**	**trying**	**vain**	wonderful
sly	stopper	**that's**	tube	**vane**	wood
smashed	stories	**their**	tunnels	vetoes	**word history**
smitten	**storybook**	theme	turmoil	**vibrant**	**world**
snapping	stout	**there**	**twice**	videos	worm
sneak	straggled	**there's**	two	visible	**worthwhile**
snuggle	strawberries	**thermal**	ugly	voiced	would
soaked	**stray**	they	ultra	waist	wrapped
soar	strike	**they'll**	**unable**	**wait**	**wrapper**
sob	string	they're	**unbalanced**	warm	wriggled
solos	stripe	they've	**unbelievable**	warmly	wring
some	striped	thieves	**uncorrected**	wart	**yawn**
someday	**struck**	**thinner**	**uncover**	**wasn't**	yellow
somehow	submitted	thinnest	underground	way	you'll
somersault	subtle	**thirty**	underpriced	way	you're
son	suddenly	thoughtful	**underrated**	**we'll**	**you've**
sound	**sufficient**	threw	undersized	we're	your
spark	**sugar**	throbbing	**understand**	we've	**zipper**
spawn	sum	through	underwater	weak	
spellings	**summertime**	**throughout**	**uneasy**	**wear**	
spicy	summit	**thumb**	uneasily	**weather**	
spine	sun	to	**unemployed**	week	
splashes	**supernatural**	toe	**uneventful**	weigh	
spoke	supper	**together**	**unfriendly**	**weight**	
spooky	**supplied**	**tomb**	**unhappiest**	weren't	
spotted	**supply**	tomorrow	**unhappy**	**west**	
spray	**supported**	too	unhook	wheelchair	
spreadable	**surrender**	torch	unicorn	**whenever**	